Praise for

"In the mid-'50s, country music met rock-and-roll, and it was called rockabilly. Jim West brings that unique time in Arizona to life in *The Phoenix Sound*. West gives the reader personal portraits of Marty Robbins, Sanford Clark, Duane Eddy, Jimmy Dell, Waylon Jennings, Buck Owens, producer Lee Hazlewood, Donnie Owens, Al Casey, Ted Newman and Jimmy Spellman, who found themselves playing the national stage, many of them given birth by honky-tonker Buddy Long and his Sunset Riders, who toured the Phoenix clubs to dirt roads and two-lane blacktop with an appropriate sign that read, 'Come dance and fight to the music of Buddy Long.' They are all alive and well and unforgettable in Jim's *The Phoenix Sound: A History of Twang & Rockabilly Music in Arizona.*"

—Jeb Rosebrook, author of *Purgatory Road*; screenwriter, *Junior Bonner*

"In 1956, a partner and I put the first all–country music radio station on the air in Phoenix, Arizona. It was called KHEP, and it was an immediate success. In addition, we were also promoting Grand Ole Opry package shows at the local Madison Square Garden nightclub in Phoenix, where we developed a huge following and packed the place to the rafters each week.

"When people like Lee Hazlewood introduced me to talents like Duane Eddy and Jimmy Dell, it was my pleasure to put them on our Saturday night shows with the Sunset Riders Band, where they received more and more exposure locally, which eventually led to recording contracts and nationwide appearances. We promoted other local, talented musicians and singers such as Al Casey, Jimmy Spellman, Buddy Long, Sanford Clark and Marty Robbins.

"The Phoenix Sound was a very influential period in music history. It certainly helped put the dusty desert town of Phoenix on the musical map. With its great mix of country and rockabilly, I was proud to help promote its creative sound and popularity."

—Ray Odom, Arizona media mogul and concert promoter

"Jim West is a longtime top radio personality whom I have known for over thirty years. His knowledge of the music business and the people in it is second to none! He is a personal friend of many of the top people in the business and has the trust and admiration of all of them. Jim's book is a terrific read and greatly adds to the history of the music that came out of the great Southwest!"

—Johnny Western, actor, singer and songwriter in Mesa, Arizona

"[In] January 1971, Buck Owens hired me to program his Phoenix radio stations KTUF and KNIX. KTUF AM was a daytimer located in Tempe, Arizona, in a small building down a dirt road, off Scottsdale Road and across from JD's Nightclub.

"KTUF/KNIX contributed greatly to the Phoenix Sound with connections to local nightclubs and the many artists who would stop by the station to promote their records. Among those artists was a young teenager, Tanya Tucker, who had her first hit, 'Delta Dawn,' at the age of thirteen. Other artists who would frequent the station were Waylon Jennings, Merle Haggard, Buck Owens (not only because he owned the station, but [also he] was still recording and touring) and just about every artist who was in town and appearing at one of the venues. They would stop by the radio station for an interview, promote their appearances and have their records played.

"Another way KTUF/KNIX was involved with the Phoenix Sound was establishing 'KTUF/KNIX Nights' at the local venues. This was a fun night for the listeners, winning prizes from the station and many times meeting an artist. This was not only fun for the listeners, but [also] helped to promote the nightclubs and the station as well.

"It was a memorable time in the radio and music industry, and for me personally, I'm grateful to have a small part in the Phoenix Sound. Thanks, Jim, for your work in sharing this wonderful bit of history, and the best of luck with your book my friend."

—Larry Daniels, former program and operations manager,
KTUF-KNIX, Phoenix

THE PHOENIX SOUND

—SOUND—

A HISTORY OF TWANG & ROCKABILLY MUSIC IN ARIZONA

JIM WEST | *Foreword by* MARSHALL TRIMBLE

THE
History
PRESS

Published by The History Press
Charleston, SC
www.historypress.net

First published 2015

Manufactured in the United States

ISBN 978.1.46711.898.9

Library of Congress Control Number: 2015952223

I dedicate this book to my children, Cody, Matt and Holly. I've always been very proud of your talents and accomplishments. Continue to aim high! I love you.
—Dad

CONTENTS

FOREWORD

The mid-1950s was a great time to be coming of age in Phoenix. I turned sixteen in 1955, a milestone coinciding with the birth of the Phoenix Sound. That was about the time music tastes of teenagers switched from Patti Page and Tony Bennett to Elvis Presley, Buddy Holly and Pat Boone.

I caught most of the country music shows that performed at the old Madison Square Garden on Seventh Avenue, including Grand Ole Opry stars like Webb Pierce, Mel Tillis and Patsy Cline. We danced to the music of country stars like Johnny Cash, Buck Owens and Marty Robbins at Sciots, an open-air pavilion on Central, just south of Indian School Road. Two other great spots for dancing and meeting girls were on Central Avenue down by the Salt River at Sarg's Cowtown and at the Riverside Ballroom.

I have the distinction of bearing witness to a fight at the Riverside before I was even born. It was the fall of 1938; my mother was about seven months pregnant when she and Dad decided to go dancing. A fight broke out, and Dad pushed Mom under a table. Naturally, I don't remember the details.

Legend has it that those Russian farm boys from nearby Glendale used to tape their hands in the parking lot like professional boxers before they went dancing at places like the Cowtown and Riverside. There was a curious irony that the band leader's last name at the Riverside was "Fite."

There were a number of home-grown, up-and-coming stars performing on local television during those years, including Al Casey, Jimmy Spellman, Duane Eddy, Sanford Clark, Ted Newman, Jimmy Dell, Donnie Owens and more.

Sarg's Cowtown club featuring Donnie Owens & the Jacks. A popular watering hole in the 1960s, it could be a rough place where the farm boys from Glendale and local cowboys would have weekly parking lot fights. *Courtesy of* True West *magazine and John P. Dixon.*

The folk music scene was also heating up and lively in Scottsdale, with performers like Dolan Ellis, Ian MacPhersen, Loy Clingman and Henry Thome. John Denver performed at the Lumber Mill club. Waylon Jennings came in on Monday's open mic night before they both hit the big time.

Jack Miller and Lee Hazlewood were doing incredibly creative things at the Ramsey's Recording Studio on Seventh Street.

All were music pioneers who would bring national recognition to the desert community that, in 1950, was the ninety-fifth-largest city in the United States. Boy, was that all about to change!

MARSHALL TRIMBLE
Arizona's official state historian

ACKNOWLEDGEMENTS

Over the past five years, many people encouraged me to write this book, and I have many people to thank for their contributions and insight. As a longtime radio broadcaster, I was always a little familiar with this musical time frame and era in Phoenix. I wrote the book out of my love of music, all kinds of music. I could never sing or play a lick, but I sure was a fan of the music and musicians who had that skill I admired and probably will never, ever have.

I'd like to thank the folks who helped make it happen, like Rock and Roll Hall of Famer Duane Eddy for embracing and trusting me with his story and for tolerating the many e-mails and phone calls to Nashville for his invaluable input. Mr. Eddy was in the thick of it when the Phoenix Sound was born.

Jimmy Dell, Duane's old running buddy, is another player from that era who offered help and guidance in telling this story. Two of the kingpins of the Phoenix Sound, and they were as humble and helpful as anyone could have been. I am grateful.

I'd like to thank Jack Miller, Grammy Award–winning engineer to the stars; Bob Boze Bell from *True West* magazine; motion picture screenwriter and author Jeb Rosebrook; and John P. Dixon for insight and for contributing many photos of the performers. I appreciate people like Dionne Hauke and her husband, Chuck, from Ziggies Music; Ray Odom; Johnny Western; Dolan Ellis; the Coolidge, Arizona Historical Society; the world-class MIM-Musical Instrument Museum; Bear Family Records; and the Buck Owens Private Foundation.

ACKNOWLEDGEMENTS

Thank you to Gary Clemmons, Tina Cox-Clemmons, John Hill, Sanford Clark, Ray Lindstrom, Claude Henry, Terri Sussman, Larry Daniels, Ted Newman, Jimmy Spellman, Beve Cole, Delcie Shultz, Karin Enloe, Al Perry and Don and Linda Brown. All made a big contribution to helping tell the Phoenix Sound story.

I'm grateful to and appreciate you all.

INTRODUCTION

Phoenix, Arizona, in the 1950s was quite a charming place to live. The 1950 census measured about 106,000 people who fit nicely into Phoenix's seventeen square miles. Ten years later, in 1960, the boom times really began; the population jumped to about 460,000, and the city fathers acquired some two hundred square miles of land. Irrigated farmland abounded just outside of town, making the Sonoran Desert green.

Citrus groves, palm trees and cotton fields prevailed. Living was slower and easier until urban sprawl took hold and someone perfected air conditioning. Today, Phoenix is the fourth-largest city in the United States with a metro population approaching five million. It is Arizona's big city.

But during the Eisenhower administration, times were simpler and innocent. Many cities would begin to develop a signature sound to their local music scenes. Some examples include the Memphis Sound, with Elvis, Johnny Cash, Carl Perkins and Jerry Lee Lewis as its star base. The Nashville Sound of country artists such as Jim Reeves, Patsy Cline, Eddy Arnold and others had emerged by the late '50s. Even tiny Clovis, New Mexico, would cultivate future stars, such as Buddy Holly, a young Waylon Jennings before he moved to Phoenix and the rock-and-roll group Jimmy Gilmer and the Fireballs, which charted a number one song at the tiny Norman Petty recording studio. Coincidentally, an old radio station boss of mine, Jim Slone, recorded several songs at the Petty studio with a doo-wop group called the Shy Guys in the early '60s.

INTRODUCTION

Phoenix, Arizona, in the 1950s—a boomtown on the horizon. *Courtesy of the author. All rights reserved.*

The Los Angeles and New York music scenes were huge and influential. We can't forget the Detroit Motown Sound and the Bakersfield Sound of West Coast country music that rivaled the Nashville Sound with a more pronounced honky-tonk twang influenced by rock-and-roll, rockabilly, southwestern cowboy music and even Mexican polkas.

Phoenix also had its own sound that drifted out of the tiny upstart recording studio known as Ramsey's on Seventh Street and Weldon, just south of Indian School Road. Some of the names associated with its future success include Lee Hazlewood, Al Casey, Sanford Clark, Duane Eddy, Jimmy Dell, Donnie Owens, Ted Newman, Skip and Flip, Dyke and the Blazers, the Tads, Ray Sharpe and many other lesser-known acts all looking for an elusive hit record.

The city and state would also be the launching ground for many future big stars and entertainers such as Rex Allen, Wayne Newton, Marty Robbins, Buck Owens, Waylon Jennings, Dolan Ellis, Linda Ronstadt, Alice Cooper, Stevie Nicks, the Gin Blossoms, Goose Creek Symphony, Tanya Tucker, LaCosta Tucker, Jessi Colter, Jerry Riopelle, Steven Spielberg and, in the past few years, country singer Dierks Bentley.

The innovation and music of the Phoenix Sound was groundbreaking. Most acts hoped for the best as they grasped for that brass ring of stardom.

INTRODUCTION

Recording technology and audio-recording tape became more and more perfected after World War II, and the sky was the limit.

People were starting to dream big. If a Memphis truck driver named Elvis Presley could make it big in show business and music, with a little luck and talent, maybe they could, too!

1
EARLY ARIZONA MUSIC PIONEERS

As we start this musical journey, there are a few pioneers who came first, paving the way for the future. A young woman led the way as one of Arizona's first musical recording pioneers.

Music in the Mountains: Billie Maxwell

In eastern Arizona, not far from the New Mexico line, is the small town of Springerville. Young Billie Maxwell came off the family ranch to become perhaps the very first cowgirl singer. At that time, songs were sung to pass the time of day. In February 1929, Billie and her family were invited to make a long, arduous trip on mostly primitive dirt roads to El Paso, Texas, to record for the Victor Record Company. It later became RCA-Victor. Billie reportedly cut four recordings, or "sides." She recorded a song called "Cowboy's Wife," full of longing for her husband to come home from the cattle drive. These early 78rpm pressings only totaled between 1,100 and 1,600 copies.

Billie Maxwell and her family band, the White Mountain Orchestra, entertained at dances all over eastern Arizona. They played music handed down in the family for generations. There is no record of any radio airplay, as radio stations were nonexistent in that part of the state at that time. Those rare Victor 78rpm Billie Maxwell discs are collector's items today and were

Billie Maxwell and the White Mountain Orchestra. Maxwell was a pioneering performer in Arizona and probably the first cowgirl singer. She recorded on the Victor label in El Paso in the 1930s with famous A&R man Ralph Peer. *Courtesy of Robert Shelton and Burt Goldblatt, the Country Music Story, Castle Books. All rights reserved.*

recorded with Victor's famous A&R man Ralph Peer. Those were the days of primitive recording techniques, of cutting a disc on a lathe. This was how they did it before the invention of audio-recording tape. Peer would roam all over the South and West looking to record regional styles of music.

Billie's music didn't sell many of the recordings made. Neither she nor her family was ever asked to record again, nor did they receive much recognition or any money for their trouble. In her own unusual style, Billie helped pave the way for future female singers. She died in 1954.

Billie Maxwell could well have been the very first female country-western singer to be recorded, even predating Ruby Rose Blevins. Ruby Rose was better known by her stage name, Patsy Montana, and her song "I Want to Be a Cowboy's Sweetheart," which was not released until 1935. Montana, though, has the distinction of being the first female country or hillbilly singer to have a million-selling record with "Cowboy's Sweetheart."

A Root Beer Stand in Phoenix

The year 1929 was also important as the year that the Arizona Wranglers began singing and playing together at the XXX Root Beer stand in Phoenix. Their original cast of characters and musicians included a guy nicknamed "Hoss-Fly," "Hungry" Joe Ivans, Charles Hunter and J.E. Patterson. Being in Phoenix, it was a given that they would perform live on either KOY or KTAR Radio.

The Arizona Wranglers were an early musical group that entertained Depression-era audiences and winter visitors in the state. *Courtesy of Robert Shelton and Burt Goldblatt, the Country Music Story, Castle Books. All rights reserved.*

They played dance halls and shows all over the state and even headed to California, where they performed over KNX Radio in Los Angeles. Many other band members joined through the years, and the Arizona Biltmore hotel became one of their favorite venues to perform at, entertaining winter visitors who came by train to bask in the sunshine and soak up some "cowboy singer" fun.

Gene Autry Joins the Army Air Corp

While he established himself as a singing cowboy on the silver movie screen during the 1930s and not as part of the Arizona music scene, Gene Autry nevertheless made his mark on the state in a big way. Autry was stationed at Luke Field (now Luke AFB) during World War II and broadcast his *Melody Ranch* radio show over local Phoenix airwaves.

Autry loved Arizona so much that after the war he would team up with businessman Tom Chauncey and purchase KOOL Radio and television and a radio and TV station in Tucson. Autry would become a huge media mogul, entertainment icon and future owner of the California Angels baseball team.

Another talented future celebrity lived in Phoenix in the 1940s, attended what was then Arizona State College (now University) and worked at KOY Radio. He later hosted an early version of television's *Tonight Show*. His name was Steve Allen.

The post–World War II era saw an increase in music venues and clubs opening in the Phoenix area. Returning GIs once stationed at the nearby air bases came back to put down roots and raise families in the green, irrigated valley. Several clubs and honky-tonks would pop up to serve middle-class, beer-drinking crowds who liked to dance.

In late 1947, Bob Fite and his Western Playboys, a fourteen-piece western swing band similar to Bob Wills and his Texas Playboys, commanded the bandstand at the Riverside Park Ballroom near the banks of the Salt River south of downtown Phoenix.

It was music for the common man—the hardworking farmer, rancher or construction or factory worker seeking a good time. Some of the major clubs of the era were the Riverside, Sarg's Cowtown, Abel Hall, Madison Square Garden, Vern and Don's, Sciots Ballroom and, later, J.D.'s, Mr. Lucky's and Handlebar J, among many others.

The Phoenix Sound is best described as a hybrid of rock-and-roll, rockabilly and country music, with a little doo-wop and maybe a hint

The Riverside Park Ballroom was a popular place to dance to Bob Fite and the Western Playboys and others in the 1950s and '60s. *Courtesy of* True West *magazine. All rights reserved.*

Bob Fite (center), Brick Herndon and the Western Playboys performed at the Riverside Ballroom. They are pictured here with singer Freddie Hart. *Courtesy of Ray Odom.*

of jazz and R&B. It was an art form at the dawn of a nationwide music revolution. Throughout this book, we'll put the spotlight on more of the better-known musical acts that helped put the dusty desert town of Phoenix on the musical map.

2

RUNNING WITH THE BIG DOGS

HAZLEWOOD, RAMSEY, MILLER

In the beginning, the term "Phoenix Sound" became descriptive when one musical success after another seemed to rise out of the local desert music scene like the proverbial phoenix bird. Floyd Ramsey's Seventh Street recording studio was in its infancy in 1954. But by 1956 and '57, it was hopping with the success of the first big record to emerge that had some staying power on the national *Billboard* magazine music charts, not only locally and regionally, but nationally as well.

One of the key figures who stood tall and proud was the driven and influential disc jockey turned songwriter and record producer Lee Hazlewood. After serving in the army in Korea, he started his first radio job at the only radio station in Coolidge, Arizona: KCKY. He was an immediate hit with the locals and would prove to be an extraordinary producer with a great track record over the years.

One day, Coolidge High School student and guitar player Duane Eddy went out to the station with another friend to meet Hazlewood, and they immediately hit it off. It wasn't long before Eddy paired up with high school friend Jimmy Delbridge, and they began performing together. In 1954, Hazlewood produced an early single with the duo: "Soda Fountain Girl" and "I Want Some Lovin' Baby." Buddy Long and his Western Melody Boys backed them up, and Hazlewood had five hundred copies pressed on his own Eb. X Preston record label. The single died a quick death with no local airplay and few sales. There was another reason for its quick demise, but more on that later.

KCKY Radio in Coolidge, Arizona, was influential in the early Phoenix Sound era and was where Lee Hazlewood and, later, Waylon Jennings were local disc jockeys. *Courtesy of Russ Jackson. All rights reserved.*

An early Coolidge, Arizona jam session, 1954. *From left to right:* Jimmy Dell on piano and Duane Eddy on guitar, along with "E.B. Lightning" McGee. Big things were on the horizon for these two Coolidge High School boys. *Courtesy of Claude and Delores Henry. All rights reserved.*

Seeking a better-paying radio gig, Hazlewood soon moved up to Phoenix to work with Ray Odom at KRUX. He began shuttling Delbridge and Eddy up to a Saturday night "Arizona Hayride" show that Odom was emceeing, and they played with the Sunset Riders band, which included musicians Buddy Long and guitarist Al Casey. It was great grass-roots exposure for all of these entertainers

Hazlewood began writing and producing music out of Ramsey's studio. Beginning in the late '40s, Floyd Ramsey and his father, Clay, were operating a small studio in the back of a radio and phonograph repair shop. There was also a barbershop and record label operating out of this nondescript building—humble beginnings that would soon explode with recording activity.

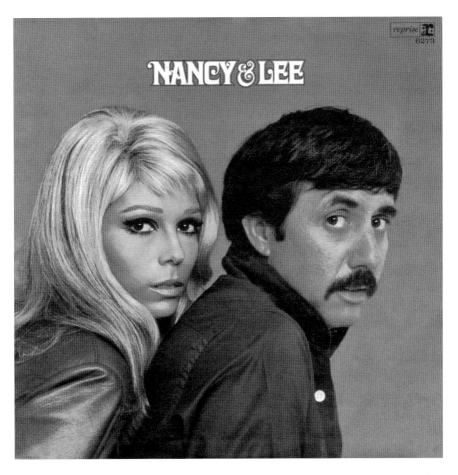

Influential record producer and songwriter Lee Hazlewood, who contributed greatly to the Phoenix Sound era and went on to even bigger success writing and recording with Nancy Sinatra. *Courtesy of Dionne Hauke and Ziggies Music. All rights reserved.*

A re-created Ramsey's recording studio on display at the Musical Instrument Museum (MIM) in Phoenix, Arizona, in a display called "I Am AZ Music." *Courtesy of the Musical Instrument Museum (MIM). All rights reserved.*

One day in 1956, Hazlewood told local guitar player Al Casey that he was seeking a young good-looking kid who could sing and asked if he knew of anyone who would fit the bill. Casey remembered old high school friend Sanford Clark and promptly got ahold of him. Clark was about to be discharged from the U.S. Air Force and was stationed out at Luke Air Force Base in nearby Glendale. In the air force, he had been in a band that, while off duty, had won a talent competition and was supposed to be featured on *The Ed Sullivan Show*, but military duties came first. Clark had been playing guitar for a few years and jumped at the chance to learn and record a new song Hazlewood had written called "The Fool."

It wasn't long before Clark recorded "The Fool" at Ramsey's. The single was first released on the local MCI label and featured Al Casey's repetitive guitar licks, which helped the song stand out from the norm. A disc jockey in Ohio told Hazlewood he had a hit record on his hands. Soon, Ramsey was leasing the master single to the DOT label, and with wider distribution across the country, it began selling like hotcakes. In the blink of an eye, the

A publicity shot of Sanford Clark after the success of the song "The Fool." Clark would record well into the 1970s on many different record labels. He and producer Lee Hazlewood recorded a lot of good music, but Clark never matched the success of that first top-ten single. *Courtesy of Sanford Clark. All rights reserved.*

single sold over 700,000 copies and reached into the *Billboard* magazine top-ten charts.

All of a sudden, the music industry was keeping an eye on the budding music scene in Phoenix. Sanford Clark began touring the country with Al Casey on the success of the song. Clark recorded many other well-written and produced songs by Hazlewood on a variety of record labels well into the '70s, but they never matched the success of "The Fool."

Lee Hazlewood moved on to California to work with DOT Records not long after the nationwide impact of "The Fool." But after a year of no

Left: Audio engineer Jack Miller at Ramsey's studio, Phoenix, 1958. Miller engineered hundreds of recording sessions, including Duane Eddy's first sessions that helped launch his "twangy guitar" sound. *Courtesy of Jack Miller. All rights reserved.*

Below: The Ampex tape deck that Jack Miller owned and which helped him secure his job at Ramsey's studios in Phoenix in the 1950s. *Courtesy of the Musical Instrument Museum (MIM). All rights reserved.*

success on the West Coast, he was back in Phoenix looking to record other acts at the Ramsey studio.

Jack Miller and his family had moved to the Phoenix valley in 1953. As a child in Chicago, he had acquired an early audio-recording device and started recording his family singing and playing music. He recorded weddings and even funerals and learned mixing techniques at an early age. Knocking on a few record label doors in Phoenix looking for work, he came up empty more times than not.

When he visited Floyd Ramsey seeking a job, Ramsey at first told him he had no openings. Miller, however, had an ace up his sleeve. He had acquired his very own state-of-the-art Ampex 350-track audio tape recorder. Ramsey did not have one. Miller told Ramsey, "I'll bring it with me if you give me a job." Ramsey suddenly had an opening.

At first, Miller was relegated to repairing radios and fixing phonographs, which he hated, but he had his foot in the door to what he really wanted to do: become a recording engineer. He soon was working in the studio with Ramsey and Hazlewood. Other producers were Connie Conway and Jimmy Wilcox.

Hazlewood asked Eddy to write a song. Eddy came back with "Moovin' and Groovin,'" his first single. His next effort proved to be huge when he recorded a song called "Rebel Rouser." Licensed to the Jamie Record label out of Philadelphia, "Rebel Rouser" exploded on the nationwide charts and eventually sold several million copies. Eddy's innovative guitar licks became known as the "twang heard 'round the world."

The hits just kept on coming. Songs like Skip and Flip's "It Was I" charted. Local ASU football star Ted Newman was seeing his song "Plaything" climb and land at number forty-five on the *Billboard* charts. Duane Eddy's high school buddy Jimmy Delbridge struck some rockabilly gold with songs like "I've Got a Dollar" and "Teenie Weenie" under the stage name of Jimmy Dell with RCA records.

The young Newton Brothers, Wayne and Jerry, did some early recordings, and country singer Waylon Jennings recorded his early music at Ramsey's, which changed its name to Audio Recorders of Arizona in 1958. A spacious new building to house the studio was constructed across the street from the original in 1964. A group called the Tads recorded some doo-wop music, and R&B group Dyke and the Blazers charted with the song "Funky Broadway," which was later covered by Wilson Pickett.

Lee Hazlewood was always looking for a creative idea and became interested in other artists' music. "Lee was the first DJ to break Elvis over the airwaves in Phoenix," said Duane Eddy. Local singer Chuck "the Eloy

Left: Sanford Clark and Duane Eddy, two of the major players of the Phoenix Sound. *Courtesy of* True West *magazine and Ray Odom. All rights reserved.*

Below: Audio Recorders of Arizona got its start as the Ramsey recording studio, where Duane Eddy, Jimmy Dell, Al Casey, Waylon Jennings and others recorded at the dawn of their respective careers. *Courtesy of Floyd Ramsey. All rights reserved.*

AUDIO RECORDERS OF ARIZONA
3830 N. 7th Street, Phoenix Arizona - Opened April, 1964

Flash" Mayfield had just come off a tour of the South with country singer Hank Snow and a young, dark-haired, polite kid from Tupelo, Mississippi, named Elvis Presley. It's reported that Hazlewood went crazy when he first heard Elvis's music and almost got fired from his radio show for playing him too much.

In 1963, Hazlewood recorded his first solo album, called *Trouble Is a Lonesome Town*—a concept album about people in a small western town with narration as well as singing. He recorded for Reprise, MGM and several other labels over the years.

His biggest success was yet to come when he moved back to Los Angeles and began producing big acts like Frank Sinatra and Dean Martin. Sinatra was looking for a producer to help jumpstart his daughter Nancy's career and tagged Hazlewood to do the job.

By the mid-1960s, big hits had come for Nancy Sinatra. Her biggest hit was the Hazlewood-penned "These Boots Are Made for Walking," and together the pair recorded duets like "Jackson," "Summer Wine" and the haunting "Some Velvet Morning."

At the end of the '60s, Hazlewood moved to Sweden and continued to write, produce and record, not only his own recordings, but other acts as well. He developed a cult-like following with his music and production techniques. With his health failing, he recorded one last album called *Cake or Death* and passed away in Las Vegas in 2007, having made quite an impact on the music scenes in Phoenix and Los Angeles—and even in Sweden, of all places.

Floyd Ramsey continued with many years of success at Audio Recorders. He owned

Lee Hazlewood in the 1950s. He produced many hit records that came out of Phoenix, including "The Fool" by Sanford Clark and "Rebel Rouser" by Duane Eddy, among many others. *Courtesy of John P. Dixon. All rights reserved.*

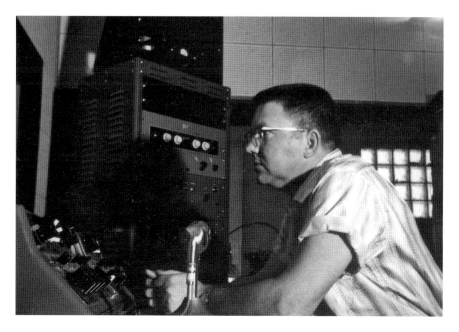

Floyd Ramsey (pictured) and his father, Clay, built the Ramsey recording studio, which later became Audio Recorders of Arizona. Most of the great music of the Phoenix Sound era was recorded there. *Courtesy of John P. Dixon. All rights reserved.*

many record label imprints, including MCI, Ramco, Liberty Bell, REV and others. He even recorded the Phoenix Symphony. In the '70s, Audio Recorders changed its name again to Audio-Video Recorders, and the business continued to thrive. Floyd Ramsey passed away in 2008.

Jack Miller continued in his role as engineer and produced hit after hit. At one point, he got the chance to move to Los Angeles and the RCA studios, where he engineered sessions with groups like the Monkees, the Rolling Stones, Henry Mancini and others. Not wanting to raise his children in the LA smog, he moved back to Arizona and picked up where he had left off at Audio Recorders. In the '80s, he opened his own studio and specialized in recording radio and television commercials. I was honored to have Jack Miller be the recording engineer on many radio and television "voice-overs" I recorded in his studio.

Miller won a Grammy Award for his Native American recordings at Canyon Records in Phoenix. When I interviewed him for this book, he was working at least part time at Canyon, still mixing and recording.

Lee Hazlewood, Floyd Ramsey and Jack Miller are three very important names associated with the Phoenix Sound. They were the big dogs.

3
THE TWANG IN THE DESERT

DUANE EDDY

Y ou'll never work in this town again!" an angry caller told a fifteen-year-old Duane Eddy, who was just starting his music career in small Coolidge, Arizona. It was 1954, and while attending high school, Eddy was growing more confident in his guitar skills. People began offering him jobs playing music in the area on the weekends. Eddy tells me that one day he received a call from Johnny, who fronted the Johnny Griffin Band, a three-piece outfit looking for a guitar player to round out the band at a gig at the local VFW hall. Eddy told him, "I know a few songs but am still learning." But after Johnny determined Eddy could hold his own in the band, he offered him fifteen dollars for his first paying job. "OK," Eddy agreed, "I'll be there Saturday night."

No sooner had he hung up the phone than it rang again with yet another gig offer. This time, sax player Benny Arnold from a society-type band offered Eddy twenty-five dollars to play at the Coolidge Country Club. Honoring the original verbal agreement, Eddy turned him down, saying he was already booked that night. "Well, call them back and tell them you can't make it, and come play for twenty-five," Arnold barked.

"I can't do that," Eddy replied. "I gave my word."

Arnold got angry and screamed, "You'll never work in this town again! And remember, my father is the mayor." He then abruptly hung up.

Duane Eddy paused for a moment and then smiled, thinking to himself that he was already a has-been before he even got started entertaining in tiny Coolidge, Arizona.

At the age of five, a young Duane Eddy noticed a guitar in the basement and asked his dad to teach him a few chords. After that, he was hooked. "The first guitar I ever bought was a 1954 Les Paul Goldtop at the local hardware store in Coolidge. It cost me something like seventy dollars, which was a lot of money to me then. I heard of a guy who built amps in the area. I didn't own one, so I bought a homemade orange crate amp with a wire grill to protect the speaker. It worked very well, and both guitar and amp served me well for the next couple of years or more," Eddy said.

He practiced, and then he practiced some more.

The Eddy family had moved to Tucson in 1951 from Upstate New York. "In Tucson, my dad got a job with Safeway stores and worked his way up. In the fall of 1953, they promoted him to manage the Safeway store in Coolidge, so we moved again."

Attending high school in Coolidge, Eddy met local KCKY disc jockey Jim Doyle. Doyle recorded Eddy playing a guitar instrumental at the station. The next day, he played the music on his radio show, and all of Coolidge heard Eddy play. Suddenly, Eddy was in demand to join pick-up bands and play the local VFW and other venues.

A young man by the name of Jimmy Delbridge heard Eddy play on the radio and promptly sought him out at Coolidge High, suggesting they start playing music together. At first, Delbridge also played guitar, but he switched to piano to accompany Eddy. The boys began playing at church, school dances, friend's homes and the Coolidge Armory. They even played in a few parades.

"One day, good friend Ed Myers took me out to the radio station to meet a guy named Lee Hazlewood," Eddy recalled. "He said, 'You've got to meet this new DJ. He is a talented and funny guy.'" Shortly thereafter, Eddy and Delbridge would record that first song Hazlewood had written. Eddy remembers, "It was 1955 [when] Lee takes us to a studio in the back of someone's house in Phoenix. I think it was called Ambassador Studios, which was a rather pretentious name for such an amateur studio. We were backed up by Buddy Long and his Western Melody Boys band in the session for 'Soda Fountain Girl' and 'I Want Some Lovin' Baby.'"

"Most of the copies of the song sat in Hazlewood's garage because my friend Jimmy went and got saved—saved in church—and decided he could not play secular music anymore. He would flip-flop back and forth and change his mind constantly." Eddy continued, "So at the time, that box of five hundred records collected dust in the garage since there was no sense in releasing it to be promoted at radio when Jimmy quit. All in all, though, it was a humble beginning."

A Sunset Riders advertisement, managed by Forrest Skaggs. *Courtesy of John P. Dixon. All rights reserved.*

In June 1955, Eddy graduated from high school and promptly left town for a job in Los Angeles, working for the local gas company for six months. "I came back to Coolidge in November," Eddy said, "and since Jimmy had back-slid again, we were able to sing once again on Odom's Hayride show in Phoenix. It was about this time that I realized I wanted to actually be a musician or recording artist."

Sunset Riders featured a young Buddy Long singing lead and Duane Eddy on guitar, plus Jimmy Dell on piano. The group would play at the Saturday night Arizona Hayrides shows at the Madison Square Garden. *Courtesy of* True West *magazine and the Duane Eddy Collection. All rights reserved.*

In 1956, guitarist Al Casey recommended Eddy to replace him on the Sunset Riders band, which played on Ray Odom's Arizona Hayride shows on Saturday nights at a venue called Madison Square Garden in downtown Phoenix. "Odom hired Buddy Long and myself at the same time," Eddy said. "Buddy was the singer, and I played guitar. We backed the talent on the Garden shows in Phoenix, played for the dance afterward and also on an hour-long TV show on Channel 3 called the *Hillbilly Hit Parade*. We then played gigs all over the Phoenix valley on the strength of that TV show.

"In 1957, I went to Ziggie's Music store in Phoenix and purchased an Orange Gretsch 6120 'Chet Atkins' model guitar equipped with a Bigsby vibrato," Eddy continued. "I had recently sold my orange-crate amp and bought a new Magnatone amp, which my father had to co-sign for both of them, as I wasn't old enough yet. But Ziggie let me take the new Gretsch with me that day even though my dad couldn't get up to Phoenix to co-sign

Ziggie Sardus opened Ziggie's Music in Phoenix in the 1920s, serving the working musician. Ziggie sold Duane Eddy his first Gretsch guitar, on which he performed "Rebel Rouser." *Courtesy of Dionne Hauke and Ziggie's Music. All rights reserved.*

the loan for two to three months. That's the way Ziggie was—a good and kind man who was a musician's friend. The store is still there in Phoenix. Ziggie is long gone, but his granddaughter Dionne Hauke runs it now."

While working at recording studios in Hollywood, Hazlewood had an "echo chamber" at his disposal. Several months before Eddy's first recording sessions and almost a year before "Rebel Rouser," Hazlewood came up with the idea of using a big water tank for an echo effect in the Ramsey studio.

"One afternoon, Lee, Jack, Floyd and I all drove down to the Salt River and yelled into water tanks," Eddy recalled. "The owner looked at us like we were crazy, but we found one that had a satisfactory echo in it. It was trucked up to the studio where it was elevated on a platform and a mic set up on one end and a speaker on the other that created that echo effect.

"That jury-rigged, homemade echo worked like a charm. The combination of that great tank echo and the echo chamber at Gold Star studios in Hollywood, where Lee over-dubbed my records and made the final mixes of them, became part of the sound that was so innovative and so successful for us in those early days." Eddy said. Later, Phil Spector created his "Wall of Sound" at Gold Star Studios.

In October 1957, Hazlewood asked Eddy to go home and write a song. Eddy came back with "Moovin' and Groovin'," and he and Al Casey co-wrote "Up and Down," In November 1957, they recorded the songs at Ramseys. "They were pressed on Jamie Records out of Philadelphia where the master tapes were sent," Eddy said. "In January 1958, the single charted at number seventy with an anchor on the *Billboard* chart. However, Jamie Records were encouraged enough to move forward with more studio work, and on March 16, 17 and 18 of 1958, I recorded the songs 'Rebel Rouser,' 'Stalkin',' 'The Lonely One' and 'The Walker.'" Hazlewood produced, and Jack Miller was the engineer.

In late April 1958, the singles "Rebel Rouser" and "Stalkin'" were released and exploded on the charts. They sold about three million copies that year. I asked Eddy where he got the idea for "Rebel Rouser."

"It came from a mental picture I had of a street gang in an alleyway getting ready to rumble with switch blades and chains," he said. In more recent years, you might have heard "Rebel Rouser" in the movie *Forrest Gump*. It is the song heard early in the film when young Forrest Gump is being chased by the bullies in the pickup truck and he breaks free of his polio ankle and leg braces and runs. "Run, Forrest, run!"

Eddy credits Hazlewood with his unique ability to get just the sound he wanted in the studio: "When Lee was a DJ for two or three years, he listened to all the hits on the good radio station speakers as they were played. He analyzed and memorized sounds he liked so later on, when we went into the studio to produce a record, he knew exactly what kind of sound he wanted to get on the bass, the drums, the sax, keyboards, guitars, etc. I believe as a result of doing that, he made some of the best-sounding records of the day." Eddy went on to say, "I think that is why those old recordings he produced of mine and Nancy Sinatra's still hold up so very well today."

Duane Eddy with his guitar in the Ramsey's Audio Recorders studios. Eddy is in the Rock and Roll Hall of Fame today. *Courtesy of the Musical Instrument Museum (MIM). All rights reserved.*

Eddy also sings the praises of Jack Miller: "Jack was a brilliant studio engineer. He was able to translate Hazlewood's ideas to reality. Somehow, Jack managed to get the right sound on tape and sound amazing."

All of the players and musicians were talented and were producing groundbreaking music in Phoenix. Among the players was a lone woman, Corki Casey O'Dell. Once married to Al Casey and a part of the Al Casey Combo, she was a respected musician who played on Sanford Clark's "The Fool" and on many of Duane Eddy's biggest records, including "Rebel Rouser," "Forty Miles of Bad Road," "Ramrod" and more. She has won many awards for her musicianship. As a matter of fact, O'Dell was inducted into the Musicians Hall of Fame in 2014, recognized as the first "rock-and-roll side chick" along with Velma Smith, the first country side lady, who played rhythm guitar on many country hits in the 1950s and '60s. That same year, Barbara Mandrell, Randy Bachman, Peter Frampton and others were also inducted. Duane Eddy is a member of the Musicians Hall of Fame, too. O'Dell is married to Kenny O'Dell, a major Nashville songwriter who has written some very familiar classic

Duane Eddy shares a light moment with Corki Casey-O'Dell in the studio. Casey-O'Dell was the very first "side chick" session musician, recording on lots of sessions for Phoenix-area singers and performers. She was also part of the Al Casey Combo. She is in the Musicians Hall of Fame. *Courtesy of the Musical Instrument Museum (MIM). All rights reserved.*

songs, such as "Behind Closed Doors" for Charlie Rich and "Mama, He's Crazy" for The Judds.

Eddy began touring extensively around the country and overseas. He played hundreds of shows with a virtual who's who of the day. He performed on all the teen shows like *American Bandstand* with Dick Clark and *Shindig*. Other Duane Eddy hits include "Because They're Young," "Ballad of Paladin" and "Dance with the Guitar Man," and he even won a Grammy for his version of "Peter Gunn." Eddy adopted the philosophy that to "develop your own style, [you should] do it with authority and let it all hang out."

There is some controversy over the song "Ramrod." It was written by Eddy's friend and session player Al Casey. There is speculation from some quarters that it is actually Casey playing guitar on the single version, even though Eddy's name is on the record. I asked Eddy directly if he'd care to clear this up. "I recorded 'Ramrod'; it is me playing," Eddy said. "I've even discussed this with Lee Hazlewood and Al's ex-wife, Corki Casey-O'Dell. Lee produced it. Corki played rhythm guitar, Bob Taylor was the drummer and my friend Al Casey played bass guitar that day. I remembered the session and remembered me playing lead guitar on the track."

"The first release was on the Ford label under my name and me playing on it. Then it was released on the Jamie label again, me playing," Eddy continued. "It was the same track both times, edited and overdubbed the second time. The third time Hazlewood released the track, he leased it to a label called Cindy Records and put someone named Johnny Rogers on the label, but it was me playing guitar on it. I have no idea why he would have done this except he owned the master tape, and maybe he was trying to make a few bucks while my Jamie Records version was hitting the charts. The music business was wild and open in those days. Al Casey and I stayed friends all his life, and he never mentioned any of this to me."

Duane Eddy continues to perform his classic "twangy guitar" in concerts around the country and the world. He is a popular draw in England and Europe and plays in many music festivals. He lives in the Nashville area today. In 2010, a massive flood roared through middle Tennessee and wiped out a warehouse that stored music instruments belonging to a variety of singers and entertainers. Many acts, including Eddy, lost thousands of dollars' worth of guitars, amps and equipment. Luckily, he keeps his favorite original Gretsch 6120 at home, and it was spared any damage.

All told, Duane Eddy has sold an estimated 100 million singles, EPs, albums and CDs over his entire career. "That figure was reached several years back," Eddy said. I asked if he had a favorite single among his musical catalogue. He replied with diplomacy: "My songs are like children. I like 'em or love 'em all for different reasons."

In 1994, Duane Eddy was inducted into the Rock and Roll Hall of Fame in Cleveland, Ohio. The night before his induction, he performed "Rebel Rouser" on the late night *Conan O'Brien Show*. O'Brien acknowledged Eddy's influence on such performers as Bruce Springsteen and other musicians and then asked him what he thought was his biggest contribution to music.

"My biggest contribution," said a smiling Duane Eddy, "is probably that I didn't sing."

4

FROM PIANO PICKER TO THE PULPIT

JIMMY DELL

L ife rolls a little slow in Coolidge, Arizona. Not much has changed in this small cotton farming town of about eleven thousand souls in the past fifty to sixty years. In the days before Interstate 10 bypassed the town, you might have gassed up in Coolidge along the old State Route 87, known as the "Beeline Highway" in some spots. The Greyhound bus made a quick stop here on the way to Phoenix or Tucson. The nearby Casa Grande Indian ruins draw the tourist trade.

But in the early to mid-1950s, things were heating up in Coolidge and around the country with this new form of music called rock-and-roll. A lot of parents didn't understand it and thought the youth of our country who liked it were doomed.

Much of the history of the Phoenix Sound began in rural Coolidge with the arrival of Lee Hazlewood and the early record he made with two local boys, Duane Eddy and Jimmy Delbridge. When starting out performing together, the boys would play around town at the VFW, at dances and even in church. Duane Eddy said, "After we performed in church, we weren't invited back because some people thought the performance was a little too rowdy. The congregation loved it, but the church elders were revolted and thought we were irreverent."

The Delbridge family had migrated to Arizona from Michigan because of Jimmy's father's debilitating arthritis. Settling in the dry desert helped soothe his symptoms, and his health recovered quickly. When Jimmy was a child, his father accidently ran him over with the family sedan, tearing the scalp off his head; for a time, it was touch and go whether he would survive. But the Delbridge family was built on faith in God, and young Jimmy recovered, although surgeries left him with scars and crossed eyes, and he developed a stuttering problem. He lived, but through the years he would overcome many setbacks.

Hooking up with his high school buddy Duane Eddy, Jimmy went along for the ride, but soon those five hundred freshly pressed records ended up in storage and got no airplay because Jimmy found religion—or a sense of guilt for singing secular music when he was raised in a deeply religious family. The Delbridge family were prominent members of the local Church of the Nazarene and still are today.

"I was real conflicted," Delbridge said. "I could not decide what I wanted to do. One day, I wanted to be a rockabilly singer and play with the band. The next, I wanted to pursue a career in the ministry. I knew I could not do both."

However, Delbridge did commit to performing with Eddy on Ray Odom's Saturday night Arizona Hayride shows at the massive Madison Square

Jimmy Dell was a talented piano player and rockabilly singer recording for RCA Records. He later became a very much in-demand evangelist. *Foreground, left to right*: Dolph Payer on drums and Jimmy Dell on piano. *Courtesy of* True West *magazine. All rights reserved.*

Garden in downtown Phoenix. The Garden was named after the venue in New York City.

Madison Square Garden would prove a popular place to see a show for the fan of country, rock-and-roll and rockabilly music. "I suppose we did play a little rockabilly music," said Duane Eddy, "but it hadn't been named that yet. The term came along about 1958 or 1959 and was a combination of hillbilly and rock-and-roll. Elvis said later that he just called it 'hopped-up country music,' which is exactly what we called it out in Phoenix at the time."

For a time, Delbridge went to high school during the week and headed up to Phoenix on the weekends to sit in and play piano in the Sunset Riders band. They'd perform on the *Hillbilly Hit Parade* show on Channel 3 first and then hit the main stage at the Garden. They were all making good money for the times—another reason to stick around and perform, at least for a while. Eddy recalled, "We'd also book ourselves in many small towns outside of Phoenix, and Jimmy would sit in with the band off and on for many occasions and then would be absent for months."

In his autobiography, *God's Grace*, Delbridge describes an important phone call he received from New York City. "Hello, is this Jimmy Dell?" the voice asked.

"No," Jimmy said, "my name is Delbridge, and I'll even spell it for you."

The caller said, "Jimmy, this is Steve Sholes, head of RCA Records in New York, and we'd like to offer you $15,000 if you'll change your name to Jimmy Dell and sign with our record label."

Now, Mr. Sholes was no lightweight record executive; he had discovered guitar player and future RCA Records producer Chet Atkins and had even negotiated Elvis Presley's contract when he left Sun Records and producer Sam Phillips in Memphis and joined the RCA label in Nashville.

"For $15,000, you can call me anything you'd like," Jimmy replied.

Floyd Ramsey leased several songs that Jimmy Dell recorded in Phoenix to the RCA label, and the next thing he knew, Dell was on the road with singers like Paul Anka, Jackie Wilson, Frankie Avalon and more on a nationwide Dick Clark road show. Dell said he was making about $1,000 a week—good money—and they paid for all of the travel, food and hotel expenses. "Twice a week, we'd stay in a hotel; other times, we'd be asleep on a big tour bus with someone's foot in your face," Dell said.

On the road, he'd sing hopped-up rockabilly tunes like "I've Got a Dollar," "Teenie Weenie," "She Won't Pet" and more. A lot of amped-up guitars and saxes were part of the mix of Dell's music.

Jimmy Dell in his musical heyday. Today, he keeps busy traveling the country and the world as an evangelist. Occasionally, he will perform some of his old rockabilly tunes on cruise ships and at shows. *Courtesy of Jimmy Dell. All rights reserved.*

On one big tour back east, Dell had his wallet stolen. Many of the seasoned performers told him to be sure and safeguard his wallet. "I was told to put it under my pillow at night," he said. Allegedly, some hotel maids were suspected of knocking on hotel room doors in the middle of the night and calling out, "Take your clothes to the cleaners?" If your wallet was in your pants pocket, the maids would reach in and help themselves.

Jackie Wilson and Sam Cooke both gave Dell $200 and would not let him pay them back. Dell said, "One night, in a hotel room, I had my wallet under my pillow and was just drifting off to sleep when, sure enough, I heard a maid knock and yell out, 'Take your clothes to the cleaners?' And then [I] watched her open the door and reach for my pants. I jumped out of bed and yelled, 'What do you want?' About scared the maid to death! I said, 'Get out of here"; she said, 'Take your clothes to the cleaners?' I said, 'No, not at three o'clock in the morning!' I literally learned a big lesson on the road and that is not to be taken to the cleaners!"

Despite his off-and-on performing of secular music, Dell said he never lost his Christian faith. In his autobiography, he admits that by 1964 he hadn't been to church in years. "One day, I was driving in the open desert from Scottsdale up to the town of Cave Creek. I got to singing 'Amazing Grace,' and tears started falling. I could barely see the road. I felt the Lord's presence with me that day telling me I needed to follow his word. I rebelled, and I told God I could not preach because I stuttered so bad and lacked confidence. I told God I'd make a fool of myself and that I had music contracts and obligations I could not just walk away from. I was arrogant and defiant," said Dell. But when he did commit to start preaching in the Nazarene Church, he swears that at that moment "God touched my tongue, and I've never stuttered since."

Today, Dell and his wife, Judy, run Jimmy Dell Ministries out of Phoenix. For the past forty-plus years, he has been in demand at churches, revival meetings and spiritual gatherings in several states and around the world. Dell has recorded many solo albums of gospel music featuring his unique piano skills. He loves to tell the good news in a sermon or a song.

Dell says, "God is my booking agent."

5
GUITAR SLINGER FOR HIRE

AL CASEY

Though born in California, Al Casey grew up and attended school in Phoenix. At an early age, he was picking guitar and playing in local bands. One of his earliest performances was with the band the Sunset Riders, which featured players like Duane Eddy, Buddy Long and Jimmy Dell. In 1955, he hooked up with Ray Odom on his Arizona Hayride show on Saturday nights that were standing room only.

One of the first recording sessions Casey played on was a rockabilly song called "Dig That Ford" by Doug Harden and the Desert Suns, a single that received some local radio airplay. He also played some hot licks on the VIV record label's "Cat Daddy" by Jimmy Johnson and the Arizona Hayriders, who in reality were the Sunset Riders.

It was Al Casey who contributed those haunting guitar licks that helped set apart the song "The Fool" by Sanford Clark and catapult it to number seven on the *Billboard* charts. He also went on tour with Clark promoting the song. Casey soon became an in-demand session player locally. He eventually became a fast part of the "A" team session players in Los Angeles known as the "Wrecking Crew."

Casey played on countless Phoenix sessions, including Jimmy Dell's "I've Got a Dollar" and others. He played on Jody Reynolds's "Endless Sleep," which reached number five on the national charts. This song was recorded in Los Angeles. Reynolds was playing in a band he formed in Phoenix called the Storms, and he told the *New Times Weekly* in 2001, "I wrote 'Endless Sleep' in 1956 right after I listened to Elvis sing 'Heartbreak Hotel' 5

Al Casey was a popular Phoenix-area guitarist and in-demand session musician with the "Wrecking Crew" in Los Angeles. Casey has played on the records of the Beach Boys, Nancy Sinatra, Jody Reynolds and many other stars. Al Casey returned to Phoenix and for many years taught guitar lessons at Ziggie's Music store. *Courtesy of John P. Dixon. All rights reserved.*

times on a jukebox." The record sold one million copies and launched the "teen tragedy" songs that followed, like "Teen Angel," "Tell Laura I Love Her," "Leader of the Pack" and others. Jody Reynolds died of cancer in Palm Springs in 2008. Al Casey also played guitar on the top-twenty-five hit "Need You" by Donnie Owens, recorded locally on the VIV label.

By 1958, in collaboration with Lee Hazlewood, Casey recorded and toured with Duane Eddy after the monster success of Eddy's "Rebel Rouser" and others that featured the groundbreaking "twangy guitar."

In the early '60s, Casey would adapt to the surfing craze that swept the West Coast and recorded a top-fifty song called "Surfin' Hootenanny." "Al Casey was the man about town," said singer Jimmy Dell. "He was one of the best guitar players around, and everyone used him on sessions."

Casey and his wife, Corki, even formed the Al Casey Combo, with which they toured and recorded. When Casey was called back to Los Angeles to do more session work, his schedule was a full one. Hazlewood used him on Nancy Sinatra's "These Boots Are Made for Walking," which walked to the top of the pop charts in 1966. He also played on the number-one Beach Boys hit "Good Vibrations."

Other hit records where you'll hear an Al Casey guitar riff include "Something Stupid" by Frank and Nancy Sinatra and Nilsson's number-six hit "Everybody's Talkin'" from the movie *Midnight Cowboy*. Casey even played on sides for Dean Martin and Elvis Presley.

For years after returning to live in Phoenix, he held court at Ziggie's Music store, where he taught guitar lessons. The many young people who took advantage of Casey's expertise certainly learned from one of the best. Al Casey passed away on September 17, 2006. He was a major player and architect of the Phoenix Sound who contributed to the success of a lot of entertainers' careers.

6

JACK OF ALL TRADES

RAY ODOM

In this chapter, you'll learn about a man named Ray Odom. Ray is eighty-six years young at the time of this writing (2015). Those years have been very kind to him. He exudes confidence and friendliness with the dulcet baritone of a trained radio broadcaster accompanied by a twinkle in his eye. Ray Odom has a deep knowledge of early country and rockabilly music. Phoenix and the desert Southwest region played a huge role in the national music scene, and Ray was in the thick of it all, mainly from a promotional standpoint. In the 1950s, he could have been dubbed the "Dick Clark" of country music with all the promotional efforts and shows he put forth. Mr. Odom was a showman, a pioneer radio station owner, a concert promoter, a mover and a shaker and a man about town.

Odom moved to Phoenix in 1951. He had been in radio in Texas since the '40s. In 1951, he had his own local radio show over KRIZ Radio. He soon moved across town to KRUX. Both of these stations in later years would be rival Top Forty rock stations, but in the '50s, they played a variety of programs and music, including country. Not long after he started at KRUX, he was approached to host and book shows at the weekly Arizona Hayride held in a warehouse-like building known as Madison Square Garden.

The Garden opened in 1929 and closed in 1979 and was originally built for boxing and wrestling matches. It was a popular place for working-class families to go see their favorite wrestlers, like Gorgeous George and Tito Montez, and many others perform. In addition, religious revivals would be held there and open to people of all colors and nationalities

Media mogul and former radio station owner and promoter Ray Odom on stage in the mid-1950s at Madison Square Garden. He hired Duane Eddy, Jimmy Dell and others for the Saturday evening Arizona Hayride shows at this popular downtown venue. *Courtesy of Ray Odom. All rights reserved.*

in the segregated '50s. Odom hosted hundreds of country music shows there in that decade. Eventually, it became an auto parts warehouse and closed in 1979 after fifty years.

Odom certainly was a "jack of all trades," as he also announced many of the wrestling matches that the Garden broadcast on local television. He admitted to me in the early years that he didn't know how to say "no" and agreed to wear many hats when asked.

For years, Odom kept busy booking acts from Nashville and Los Angeles. "I brought people like Frank Sinatra, Jim Reeves, George Jones and my life-long friend Ray Price, who passed away in 2014 after an incredible sixty-five-year show business career," Odom said.

He was the promoter who brought Elvis Presley into Arizona on several occasions. The very first time he booked Elvis was at the Arizona State Fair, at the rodeo arena, which held about ten thousand people. The cost to book the King was $10,000, and the price went up each and every time Odom

51

booked him in Phoenix or Tucson. There was one occasion when Presley's manager, Colonel Tom Parker, demanded and received forty uniformed police officers to surround the stage to keep the screaming teenagers at bay. It was an incredible sight. Odom told me he did not have to do much advertising, as word of mouth about Elvis coming to town always ensured a sold-out show.

Besides the big-name entertainers, Odom also booked talented local acts, and he certainly had the cream of the crop with people like Duane Eddy, Jimmy Dell, Buddy Long, Al Casey, Sanford Clark, Jimmy Spellman, Marty Robbins, the Newton boys, Wayne and Jerry, Donnie Owens and many others.

In addition to appearing on the local *Lew King Rangers* TV show, a young Wayne Newton (left) and brother Jerry (right) recorded early music in Phoenix after moving to Arizona from Ohio. *Courtesy of John P. Dixon.*

Besides promoting and booking acts on television and at the Garden's live shows, he also began bringing acts into the Riverside Park Ballroom on South Central Avenue. "We brought in Patsy Cline and a young Willie Nelson when he looked like an insurance salesman with short hair," Odom recalled. "I even brought in Johnny Cash and fan-favorite Johnny Western, who wrote the 'Ballad of Paladin' for the TV show *Have Gun, Will Travel*. If the act was popular, or up and coming, I probably booked 'em."

Odom partnered with a businessman named A.V. "Bam" Bamford and put the very first all–country and western radio station on the air in Phoenix. KHEP was a daytime-only station in 1955 but quickly built a strong audience. Among the first entertainers on his radio show at KHEP were young Wayne and Jerry Newton.

Over the years, Odom started up and owned or managed other radio stations, including KHAT in Phoenix and KMOP in Tucson, plus stations in Texas. In the early '60s, when singer Waylon Jennings hit town, he pulled a DJ shift at Odom's KHAT Radio after a short stint at KCKY in Coolidge. Odom also managed KJJJ radio in Phoenix in the '70s and '80s. When I was at Buck Owen's KNIX in the '80s, our direct competition was KJJJ.

In addition to his illustrious radio and media career, Ray Odom found time for another passion: horses. He has raced many winning Thoroughbreds

Ray Odom is still very active in retirement and was living in Sun City, Arizona, in 2015. *Courtesy of the author. All rights reserved.*

at tracks around the country, including the famous Turf Paradise track in Phoenix. Odom rode his horses in rodeo parades for many years. In retirement, he still races horses with his wife, Dolly.

Odom relishes the hundreds of stories he has of those glory days in the entertainment industry and the talented people who contributed to the Phoenix Sound. He recalled, "The city tore down the old Garden in 2006." There is a small museum tucked into a corner of the new office building there along Seventh Avenue that spotlights those days.

"Madison Square Garden was quite an exciting place to see a show. We'd pack 'em in every weekend," Odom said. Ray Odom enjoyed being in the middle of that spotlight.

7
DOING THINGS HIS WAY

WAYLON JENNINGS

The land around Littlefield, Texas, is tabletop flat. There are no mountains or hills for miles. The land is part of the *Llano Estacado*, Spanish for "staked plains," a foreboding place for early travelers due to lack of water. These plains extend from eastern New Mexico into the panhandle of Texas. It's a hardscrabble land. People who live here are hardworking farmers, ranchers and oil field hands carving out a living in a place that gets little rainfall.

Waylon Jennings was born in Littlefield in 1937. At the age of eight, his parents gave him a Harmony guitar, and he is self-taught with some help from his mother. He sought to play music to avoid picking cotton in the fields in the heat of summer.

Forming his own band at age twelve, he auditioned for a thirty-minute radio show over at KVOW in Littlefield, where he worked as a DJ, and he would later move to spin records at KDAV and KLLL in Lubbock. Jennings's musical influences were Bob Wills, Ernest Tubb, Hank Williams and Elvis.

In 1958, Jennings met Buddy Holly in Lubbock. Holly had been recording for Norman Petty at his tiny studio in Clovis, New Mexico. Jennings persuaded Holly to produce a couple songs at the Petty studios, where he recorded the song "Jole Blon" with Tommy Allsup on guitar and King Curtis on sax. Released in 1959 on Brunswick Records, it barely made a dent in the music scene.

Needing some cash flow, Holly agreed to a tour of the upper Midwest in the brutal winter of 1959. Holly had been recording in New York City and had left behind his Crickets band in Clovis. Holly hired Jennings (to play bass) and Tommy Allsup for the Winter Dance Party tour. Also along for the ride were J.P. Richardson, known as the "Big Bopper" who scored with "Chantilly Lace," and Richie Valens from California, on the bill singing his hits "La Bamba" and "Oh Donna."

In a well-documented story, the group had been zigzagging all over the upper Midwest in a drafty old bus. After the show at the Surf Ballroom in Clear Lake, Iowa, Holly chartered a small plane to fly to the next show in North Dakota when tragedy struck and the plane crashed, killing Holly, Richardson and Valens.

Devastated by the tragedy, Allsup and Jennings pulled themselves together to complete the shows for two more weeks. After that, they went back to Texas to regroup and decide what to do next. "Holly was Jennings's mentor," said Arizona State University professor Karin Enloe, who has studied southwestern music styles. "Holly had encouraged Jennings to stick up for himself and be confident. Now that mentor was gone."

Moving to rural Coolidge, Arizona, in the early '60s, Jennings landed a gig for fifteen dollars a night at the Gallopin' Goose nightclub after local band members Claude Henry and Bill Stevens invited him on stage to perform in a band that became the Ramblers. Jennings also parlayed his radio experience into a gig at KCKY, the same radio station where Lee Hazlewood had worked and discovered the talents of Duane Eddy and Jimmy Dell just a few years earlier.

Jennings's time in Coolidge was short, as he moved on to Phoenix to work for Ray Odom's KHAT Radio and formed a band called the Waylors, which played local watering holes like Frankie's in Phoenix and Wild Bill's up in north Scottsdale. (Wild Bill's later became Handlebar J, owned by Brick and Gwen Herndon and family, including musical sons Ray, Ron and Rick, who also performed at an early age.)

In 1963, Jennings moved to Los Angeles for a short time as a record producer and to record on the new A&M label, which was being formed by Herb Alpert and Jerry Moss. Alpert released a song from Jennings that was more pop-flavored than it was country. Alpert was looking to develop the first country-crossover act. "Herb Alpert heard me as singer Al Martino, but I was leaning more toward Flatt and Scruggs," Jennings said in a video biography. At one point, Jennings was quoted as saying, "I couldn't go pop with a mouthful of firecrackers."

In 1964, Jennings returned to Phoenix and hit pay dirt. A new nightclub was being opened in the river bottom area of Scottsdale and nearby Tempe.

The Gallopin' Goose nightclub in Coolidge, Arizona, was an early haunt of Waylon Jennings with a band called the Ramblers when he first hit town. The Goose has been open since 1935 and is still an active nightclub in Coolidge. *Courtesy of the author. All rights reserved.*

J.D.'s nightclub featured rock-and-roll in the basement and country music upstairs. Waylon Jennings commanded the bandstand for years and even helped design the club. KTUF Radio was owned by singer Buck Owens. *Courtesy of Jim Musil Jr. All rights reserved.*

Businessman James D. Musil opened J.D.'s nightclub. It was a cutting-edge club, and Jennings helped design it.

The nightclub became a huge success. "We were right by Arizona State University in Tempe," Jennings said. "We played songs the cowboys liked, as well as the students, professors and baseball players. Everybody got along, which is how I realized that music can be a common denominator that draws people together."

J.D.'s was built on two levels, a rock-and-roll downstairs that fit about three hundred people and a country upstairs that could hold about three times that many. Waylon and the Waylors signed as the house band and held court over a very popular run. Along with Richie Albright, Paul Foster and Jerry Gropp, they packed the place at least six nights a week. "I was making a lot of money at J.D.'s," Jennings told KNIX Radio. "It took me a long time to make that kind of money on the road, but you have to get in front of a crowd and the people who'll buy your records"

Jennings continued to hone his very unique sound with aggressive Telecaster guitar, heavy drums and incredible vocals. His sound was a mix of country, rockabilly, rock and, early on in his career, folk music.

While Jennings was playing the popular gig at the river bottom club, he headed down to Audio Recorders and recorded an album, *J.D.'s Waylon Jennings*, on the BAT record label. The album was sold at the club. It is a collector's item today and, depending on its condition, can demand big money.

With endorsements from both singer Bobby Bare and Duane Eddy, Jennings ended up being signed to RCA Records by Nashville producer and executive Chet Atkins. "Waylon and I became fast friends when I met him at

Waylon Jennings and the Waylors on stage at J.D.'s club in Tempe, Arizona, in the mid-1960s. *From left to right*: Jerry Gropp, Jennings and Buddy Long, who would play and tour with the group for a time. Paul Foster and Richie Albright would round out the early Waylors band. *Courtesy of* True West *magazine and the Buddy Long collection. All rights reserved.*

J.D.'s club one night," said Duane Eddy. "A week or so later, I ran into Chet Atkins at the RCA studios in Hollywood. I was signed to the label at that time. Talking with Chet, I also told him about Jennings's talents." Chet said, "Oh yes, Bobby Bare had mentioned him to me, but I haven't had the time to get to see him perform. Why don't we fly to Phoenix and see him?" But on the morning they were to leave for Arizona, Atkins called Eddy and said he had an emergency in Nashville and had to go back east.

Atkins told Duane Eddy, "Have Jennings call me tomorrow, and I'll send him some money to fly to Nashville and he can audition then." Waylon made that call and Chet sent him money, but instead of flying to Tennessee, Jennings packed up his car and band and drove back, set up his instruments and auditioned for Chet. By the end of the day, Jennings had an RCA contract.

There was only one small problem: Jennings was still technically signed to A&M Records in California. Herb Alpert and Jerry Moss knew that RCA could do good things for his career, so they traded his publishing for a couple years in exchange for getting out of the A&M contract. "They were good guys for negotiating that deal," Duane Eddy said.

It wasn't long before Jennings became a little frustrated. The very conservative Nashville music establishment dictated and ran tight rules in the recording studio. No road band members could play, only studio musicians, and most acts could not even pick the songs they were to record. You were told what to sing and how to sing it. Jennings said, "They would rotate producers for my sessions, and after laying down many tracks, I'd come back in and listen later and not even recognize my music. The label had changed the sound."

It was the era of the Nashville Sound, and producers like Chet Atkins and Decca Records' Owen Bradley virtually "de-twanged" the music to compete with rock-and-roll. Fiddle and pedal steel guitar almost disappeared. Instead, lush strings, piano and background singers emerged behind an awful lot of country music in the '60s.

Jennings and friends like Willie Nelson and Tompall Glaser would have none of it and began a rebellion that would revolutionize the way music was done in Nashville by the mid-'70s. Jennings was about to hang it up and quit. Jennings's drummer, Richie Albright, reportedly talked him into giving it one last try. "Try doing things your way," Albright told him.

Fearing Jennings would go to another label at the end of his contract, RCA renegotiated and gave him a nice advance with the stipulation that he could finally have artistic control in the recording studio. In 1973, Jennings released *Honky-Tonk Heroes*, a sparsely produced album with a bunch of great

Waylon Jennings's RCA Records publicity photo. The record label marketed him as "folk-country" in the beginning of his career to try to establish a niche. Jennings, however, would march to his own drummer and ultimately control his career, helping to bring about change to the way things were done in the Nashville studios. *Courtesy of Dionne Hauke and Ziggies Music. All rights reserved.*

songs written by Texas songwriter Billy Joe Shaver. "I like things that aren't perfect," Jennings told author Bruce Feiler for his book *Dreaming Out Loud: Garth Brooks, Wynonna Judd, Wade Hayes and the Changing face of Nashville.* "I want my music on the edge with some feeling in the rhythm section." Nashville was ripe for change by the mid-'70s. "We didn't need Nashville," Jennings told Feiler. "Nashville needed us!"

In 1974, Jennings scored his first number-one single with "This Time," and in 1976, a landmark album was produced. It was called *Wanted—The*

Outlaws and became the very first multiplatinum-selling album in the history of the genre. It featured Waylon Jennings, Willie Nelson, Tompall Glaser and Jessi Colter, Waylon's wife.

Hit after hit began climbing the charts with Jennings's "Luckenbach, Texas," "Are You Sure Hank Done It This Way" and "Mamas, Don't Let Your Babies Grow Up to Be Cowboys." Jennings also had hits with several duets with Jessi Colter.

With all of the successful years of recording and touring, Jennings fell into the drug scene. In 1984, he kicked the habit. In a candid interview with KNIX Radio in Phoenix in the '80s, Jennings said, "I was really bad into the drug scene. I knew I was killing myself. When I got some clarity, I could see what it was doing to my family. Drugs cost me all the way down the line. I withdrew from society, my family and myself. You become drugs." But to his credit, he came clean. Jennings also went back to school to get his GED, wanting to set an example for his young son, Shooter. Despite being a big star, Jennings was known to be generous to his friends, loved kids and adored his wife, Jessi, who stood by him for years.

Waylon and Jessi moved back to Arizona in the '90s and lived in the Phoenix suburb of Chandler. His health began declining, and he passed away in his sleep in February 2002. He is buried in the Mesa, Arizona city cemetery. The funeral was attended by many family friends and musicians coming to pay their respects. Country music had lost a legend.

Waylon Jennings charted fifty-four albums, of which eleven reached number one. He also had sixteen number-one hit singles out of ninety-six that charted in his career. He was inducted into the Country Music Hall of Fame and later honored with the Pioneer Award from the Academy of Country Music in Los Angeles. In 2005, Jennings was inducted into the Arizona Music and Entertainment Hall of Fame, leaving no doubt that he made a huge impact on the country music scene, starting in the Southwest and then taking his career to its zenith.

In that KNIX Radio interview, Jennings also stated how much he loved Phoenix. "Phoenix is good for me. I love the climate, love the people. I love the feel of Phoenix," he said.

Waylon Jennings's iconic star began to rise as part of the local music scene at a nightclub on a dusty desert street in suburban Phoenix. The crowds went wild for him then. The former J.D.'s nightclub building is still standing. Today, it is a furniture store. Local commuters drive past it daily, more than likely unaware of the music history made in that building. If walls could only speak, what tales they'd tell of those creative and groundbreaking days!

8

VIPs

VERY IMPORTANT PLAYERS

There was so much talent that came out of Phoenix and the state of Arizona. Some of the following singers, songwriters and actors predate the beginnings of the Phoenix Sound, but they all went on to attain stardom locally, nationally and internationally. Most of them started their careers in Arizona.

The "Arizona Cowboy": Rex Allen

In any talk about famous old cowboy singers, you can't exclude Elvie "Rex" Allen from the conversation. Rex was a true-blue western singer and acting icon from Arizona who rode across the silver movie screen hot on the footsteps of Gene Autry and Roy Rogers. Baby boomers might remember him as the "last of the silver screen cowboys" of a bygone era.

Before he signed a contract with Republic Pictures in Hollywood to film nineteen B movie westerns in the early 1950s, Allen already had a successful radio and singing career. Born in 1920 on a desert ranch not far from the cow town of Wilcox, Arizona, Rex started playing fiddle with his dad. Then he picked up a guitar and would roam up and down Railroad Avenue in Wilcox playing for nickels and dimes.

In young adulthood, he ventured to Phoenix for a short gig at KOY Radio. One break led to another, and Allen landed in Chicago on the *National Barn*

Rex Allen, the "Arizona Cowboy" from Wilcox, was a singer and cowboy actor of B movie westerns at Republic Pictures in Hollywood. He followed in the footsteps of Gene Autry and Roy Rogers and was the very last of the silver screen cowboys. *Courtesy of Larry and Delcie Shultz. All rights reserved.*

Dance radio show broadcast over powerful Clear Channel WLS. This was the perfect station for his singing talent. Next up was his own radio show over a nationwide CBS network.

In 1949, Allen left Chicago and struck out for Hollywood. Signing with Mercury Records, he started a successful country-western recording career. Later switching to the Decca label, he continued to record great music, including "Crying in the Chapel," which Elvis would later cover.

Gene Autry and Roy Rogers were winding down their singing cowboy acting careers, and Allen auditioned and signed a Republic Studio's contract.

His first movie was called *The Arizona Cowboy*. From 1950 to 1954, he rode across the silver movie screen on "Koko, the miracle horse of the movies" and was a Saturday afternoon matinee favorite. When his movie career ended, he starred in his own TV western called *Frontier Doctor*.

"Have you ever thought about doing movie narration work?" asked Walt Disney upon meeting Rex Allen and hearing his big baritone voice. Allen ended up narrating hundreds of Walt Disney films, including *Charlotte's Web* and *Charlie the Lonesome Cougar*.

For over sixty years, the town of Wilcox in southern Arizona has celebrated Rex Allen Days, honoring the town's most famous son. Wilcox welcomes tourists to visit the Rex Allen and nearby Marty Robbins Museums right off Interstate 10.

Rex Allen passed away in 1999 at age seventy-eight. His ashes are scattered in Railroad Park, across the street from the museum that bears his name and right next to a bronze statue of the singer. Close by is the grave of Koko, his beloved movie horse.

Marty Robbins: Arizona Native Son

With a voice second to none, Marty Robbins cut a musical pathway that started in Phoenix, and he never looked back. Born in Glendale, Arizona, his family knew deep poverty, and growing up, he developed a tough, strong work ethic in order to survive and support his family. The family did some hard labor jobs to put food on the table, including working the fields picking cotton and other drudgery work. Marty's twin sister, Mamie, said he was a fun-loving brother and that together they made their own fun in the desert as kids. At the start of World War II, Marty enlisted and was sent overseas. While off duty, he began to pick guitar with some buddies, and he found he was good at it.

In postwar Phoenix, Robbins took on many jobs, including driving a truck, digging ditches and picking cotton and citrus. Eventually, he picked a guitar instead of oranges and was able to stay out of the hot Arizona sun. He began playing local-area watering holes under the name Jack Robinson so his mother wouldn't know what he was doing; he was worried she might not approve of his making a living "in the bars."

"Marty was quite a character," said former radio station owner Ray Odom. "He was a good singer but in his early years was incredibly shy.

Martin David Robinson became Marty Robbins from Glendale, Arizona. He predated the Phoenix Sound, but not by much. He signed with Columbia Records and joined the Grand Ole Opry in Nashville. He was one of the most beloved country music entertainers. He passed away in 1982 at age fifty-seven, mere weeks after being inducted into the Country Music Hall of Fame. *Courtesy of Columbia Records and John P. Dixon. All rights reserved.*

When he played with local singer Frankie Starr at clubs like Vern and Dons or Fred Kare's place, he sometimes could not even speak on the microphone he was so shy and lacked confidence."

One time, Starr asked Robbins to tell the audience that the band was going to take a short break. He stepped up to the microphone and froze, choked up and could not speak. Realizing that this could handicap his singing career, Robbins forced himself to become more outgoing and confident.

Robbins landed his own local Phoenix radio show by walking into the radio studio one day and telling the program director that the "cowboy singer" they had on the air "wasn't very good." He boldly told the man he thought he could do better. Robbins also had his own TV show, *Western Caravan*, over channel 5 as well.

One day, Grand Ole Opry singer "Little Jimmy" Dickens came to Phoenix as part of an Opry package road show and caught Robbins's performance. In 1983, I interviewed Dickens on my show over KNIX Radio in the wake of Robbins's death in late 1982. Dickens could see and hear something special about Robbins. He contacted Columbia Records and suggested it sign him to a recording contract. Soon, there was an invitation to sign with the label, and by the early 1950s, Robbins had joined the Opry in Nashville. He was a versatile singer who could sing a variety of styles, including country, rock-and-roll, Spanish and even Hawaiian music. Robbins could have sung the phone book—he was that good.

Marty Robbins was a son of the Southwest, and the Sonoran Desert is in his DNA. He loved coming home to Phoenix from Nashville and would always get the "itch" to write a song when he started seeing the desert come into view. He never forgot his roots. His paternal grandfather was a grizzled old former Texas Ranger by the name of "Texas Bob" Heckle, and he would tell young Marty lots of tales of the Old West. This, in turn, influenced him to record one of the very first "concept" record albums. In 1959, Columbia Records released *Gunfighter Ballads and Trail Songs*, an album of western music that spawned two of his biggest hit records: "El Paso" and "Big Iron." The song "El Paso" became the very first country-western song to be honored with a Grammy Award, so Robbins was breaking new ground. Marty told Bio.com, "I'm not a real good musician, but I can write a song pretty well. I experiment once in awhile to see what I can do. I find out the best I can do is stick with writing ballads."

Robbins loved "mugging" and performing for the Opry crowds, and his fans loved him back. He branched out to his own syndicated TV series, wrote a book and even tried his hand at acting in several westerns shot at the old Apacheland movie ranch east of Mesa, Arizona. Other hit records included "Carmen" and "Ribbon of Darkness," and he scored his second Grammy Award with the song "My Woman, My Woman, My Wife," written about his wife, Marizona Robbins. Yes, that actually was her name.

About 1970, he began to experience some health problems and soon became one of the very first people in the country to undergo what was then experimental heart bypass surgery after suffering his first heart attack. He soon recovered and resumed a grueling schedule of touring, recording and even partaking in his hobby of stock car racing. He drove a few NASCAR tracks, including Talledega and Daytona. He competed with the big boys.

Robbins was still having hit records into the early 1980s, and then three major events took place before the end of the year 1982. First, he had a small part in a Clint Eastwood movie called *Honky Tonk Man*. Then he was inducted into the Country Music Hall of Fame, and finally he had his third heart attack in less than thirteen years. This time, he wouldn't recover. Marty Robbins passed away December 8, 1982, at the young age of fifty-seven. Country music fans around the world mourned his loss.

It was unfortunate, but for several years, the city of Glendale, Arizona—Robbins's hometown—seemed to forget about his achievements in the music industry. The political climate in the town included a mayor who didn't know who Robbins was and didn't seem to care and others who considered Robbins to be just a musical footnote from the past—some old hillbilly singer who had left town years ago.

In 2014, Marty Robbins finally got his due recognition in Glendale. A collaboration between the Glendale Historical Society, Juanita Buckley and her Friends of Marty Robbins organization and a longtime business in Glendale called Hickmans Egg Ranch, whose principal owners knew Marty when he was living, erected a beautifully designed plaque in Murphey Park in downtown Glendale. A new mayor, Jerry Weiers, had recently taken office and was immediately inundated with calls and requests from longtime residents claiming that it was time to honor Robbins. In September of that year, the ceremony was held. Robbins's only son, Ronnie, even attended and spoke to the crowd.

Robbins once told a TV interviewer that he was grateful that Little Jimmy Dickens had come through Phoenix with the Grand Ole Opry show and was sold on his talents, leading to his being signed to Columbia Records and the launch of his career. "So if you don't like my music, blame Little Jimmy Dickens," Robbins said with a big old grin on his face.

Buck Owens: Singer, Businessman, Hall of Famer

Taking a page out of the great American novel *Grapes of Wrath* by John Steinbeck, the Owens family of Sherman, Texas, set out during the Great Depression to see the promised land—California—in their windshield.

However, the hitch on their home-built trailer had broken several times during the long trip, and it was beyond repair when the family of ten limped into Phoenix, Arizona, in 1937.

With relatives in suburban Mesa, the family settled and began doing what they knew best: working in the fields picking cotton and oranges and performing other farm labor. Young Alvis Edgar Owens had long proclaimed that he be addressed as "Buck," the same name as the family mule. As a young man, he worked in a variety of jobs, including a stint as a Western Union telegraph delivery boy, running his own paper route with the *Arizona Republic* newspaper, driving a truck and working backbreaking labor, along with his family, in the cotton fields and orange groves. He knew there had to be a better life. He hated poverty, and he eventually would do something about it.

According to his autobiography, *Buck 'Em*, Owens began playing mandolin and a guitar and found he was a natural and learned quickly. Forming a duo with another young man, they became known as Buck and Britt and landed their own short radio show over local station KTYL in the 1940s. Owens later played in a band called Mac's Skillet Lickers, where he met his future wife, Bonnie. Soon, he was playing a variety of bars and rough roadhouses all over central Arizona, and not long after, he became a father to two young sons, Buddy and Michael. Buck Owens got his start in the country music business while a young man in Mesa, Arizona.

A relative in Bakersfield, California, told Owens there was a thriving club scene with live country music six or seven nights a week in that central California oil and farming community and said he ought to come check it out.

So by 1951, Owens had packed up and finally moved on to the Golden State, where he began playing in the nightclubs in Bakersfield, including the famous Blackboard Café & Club. It was there that he honed his guitar and singing skills. It was a rough-and-tumble way to make a living, as the West Coast crowds wanted to hear their music loud and fast in between dodging a few flying beer bottles in an occasional bar brawl.

To supplement his meager income in the clubs, Owens began commuting back and forth to Hollywood and became a studio musician at the Capitol Records Tower Studios. There he played guitar for established artists such as Tommy Collins, Faron Young, Ferlin Husky, Wanda Jackson and even rocker Gene Vincent. Owens eldest son, Buddy, told me in an interview that, early on, "my dad was invited to come down to Hollywood and play, not sing, but play guitar behind a lot of people in the studio."

Buck Owens began his music career in the mid- to late 1940s in Mesa, Arizona. By the late '50s, his Buckaroos band would begin to dominate the country music charts nationally. The band charted nearly fifty top-ten hits, including twenty-one number-one songs in *Billboard* magazine. *Courtesy of author. All rights reserved.*

Buck had developed his own unique twisted-note guitar style. It was a little off center but unique and fresh. By 1957, Capitol Records producer Ken Nelson, who had hired Owens as a sideman in the studio, offered him a recording contract when rumor had it that another label was interested. Owens's first Capitol single was a flop and generated little interest.

Believing he'd had his shot and failed, Owens asked Nelson to cancel his contract. He then headed up to Tacoma, Washington, to be part owner of a small AM radio station, play nightclubs and, before long, host his own local country television show. One good thing that came out of living in Washington State was that Owens met and hired a young fiddle player by the name of Don Ulrich. This association would be beneficial in the future.

Ken Nelson at Capitol had no intention of canceling Owens's recording contract, however, and soon invited him back to Hollywood to record several songs—such as "Second Fiddle" and "Under Your Spell Again"—that began to climb the charts. By 1959, several of Owens's singles had hit the top ten on the *Billboard* charts. Owens soon divested his business interests in Tacoma and moved back to Bakersfield.

Over the next decade and more, Owens developed his style, which expanded on the Bakersfield Sound of twangy Telecaster guitars and heavy doses of fiddle and pedal steel. It was country music with a little bit of a rock-and-roll edge to it. The West Coast Sound was counter to what Nashville had been producing, which involved de-twanging the music with background singers, piano and all-but-muted steel guitar and fiddle to appeal and sell to a more middle-of-the-road consumer.

The Bakersfield Sound stylings of Buck Owens and Merle Haggard were widely successful and offered an alternative to Nashville's brand of country. Starting with "Act Naturally," Owens and his band, the Buckaroos, rolled out number-one hit after number-one hit. They had fifteen number ones in a row at one point, and all together, Owens had twenty-one number-one records and another twenty-six that hit the top ten.

Buck Owens, Don Rich and the Buckaroos spread the West Coast, or Bakersfield, country "freight train" sound far and wide, including landmark live albums recorded at the White House, in Japan and Norway and at Carnegie Hall. Owen's music career had its humble start in Mesa-area roadhouses, where he played for tips. *From left to right*: Tommy Brumley on pedal steel guitar and Don Rich and Buck Owens on Fender Telecaster guitars. *Courtesy of the Buck Owens private foundation. All rights reserved.*

Fiddle player Don Ulrich, who went by the stage name Don Rich, moved to Bakersfield to join Owens in the studio and on the road and quickly learned Owens's unique guitar style. Owens had probably the best-sounding bunch of musicians in the '60s, including Rich on lead guitar and fiddle, Tommy Brumley on pedal steel guitar, Willie Cantu on drums and Doyle Holly on bass guitar.

Speaking of bass guitar, Ken Nelson and Owens purposely toned down the bass on recordings produced in the Capitol studios. Having worked in radio, Owens was well aware of the bass-y bottom end on mono AM radio, and he and Nelson would mix his records on small speakers like you'd have in your car to gauge how they would sound. Because of this, Owens's music had a clearer sound, and his music would seem to jump out of a car speaker with his "freight train" up-tempo beat. They turned down the bass and turned up the treble. Most of his early recordings have little bass.

Buck Owens was also a successful businessman as well as a star. He owned land, a recording studio, a talent booking agency and, for years, Bluebook, a music publishing company that housed rights to the catalogues of not only Owens's music but also most of Merle Haggard's early hit music and others who were signed to the Owens's booking agency. In 1975, Owens successfully negotiated with Capitol Records to gain ownership of all of his master recordings. Not many entertainers had the clout to be able to achieve that goal. Most record labels held an artist's music in perpetuity.

Tragedy struck in 1974 when Buck's "right arm," Don Rich, was killed in a motorcycle accident on California's Pacific Coast Highway on the way to meet his family for a vacation on the coast. Country audiences were devastated, and so was Owens; it affected him for the rest of his life.

Owens owned KUZZ Radio in Bakersfield and KTUF (later KNIX-AM) and KNIX-FM in Phoenix; he had invested in them in the 1960s. When I was employed at the station from the late 1970s to 1987, Owens would visit all of us about once per year. I had Buck on my show on several occasions. He had a great sense of humor and was quick with a joke. We spoke about his early days in Mesa. "We used to pass a soup bowl around the local bars we'd play," Buck said. "If we were lucky, we'd split eight to ten dollars in tips. Not much money, but we'd be grateful to make that." I asked if he had any regrets about the way things turned out in his career. "I wouldn't have changed a thing," Owens replied.

Buck Owens helped change the face of modern country music. On March 25, 2006, he was supposed to play a show at his Crystal Palace Nightclub and Museum in Bakersfield. He wasn't feeling well and told

The author and singer Buck Owens at a KNIX Radio station event at Mr. Lucky's club in Phoenix, 1982. *Courtesy of the author. All rights reserved.*

the band he was going to cancel and go home early. Before he could get to his car, he met an excited family who had just driven down from Oregon to see him perform. Not wanting to disappoint them, he went back into the club and played with the Buckaroos, apologizing for being sick. He soldiered through a performance for some ninety minutes. When he finished that night, he finally went home to his ranch north of town and died in his sleep.

Ironically, Buck Owens left this world exactly forty years to the day after his iconic performance with the Buckaroos at the famous Carnegie Hall in

New York City. The concert was recorded for Capitol Records that night and is one of the best live recordings ever made. The date was March 25, 1966. Buck Owens was a consummate pro to the very end.

Johnny Western: The Epic Western

Singer Johnny Western realized a dream in the entertainment industry and reaped the benefits for more than sixty years. He'll tell you he's been a very lucky man.

Johnny Westerlund, his given name, was raised in Northfield, Minnesota, the scene of the famous bank raid by Jesse James and his notorious band of outlaws in 1876. Western's love of cowboys and Indians and western music began at age five, when his parents took him to see his idol, Gene Autry, ride across the silver movie screen at a birthday party. Little did he know at the time that he'd be working for Autry as an adult.

At age thirteen, he was singing on local radio and soon became the youngest radio disc jockey in the country at KDHL in Northfield. The first song he recorded was called "The Violet and the Rose."

An early thrill was actually getting to interview his cowboy heroes—including Gene Autry, Rex Allen and Tex Ritter—on TV. "Mr. Autry told me if I ever came to Hollywood, he'd try and help me out," Western recalled. By 1955, he had moved to California and was entertaining a group of friends. He played before Roy Rogers, Dale Evans and the Sons of the Pioneers. Gene Autry was in the audience that night, and soon Western was offered a position in Autry's band. "On one tour, we played to over three million people in just fourteen days," said Western.

In 1957, Gene Autry retired from touring to concentrate on his radio and television empire, but true to his word, he hooked Western up with an agent and some acting lessons. Western acted in his first pilot for a TV show called *Pony Express*, which led to him acting in thirty-seven feature western films and in TV shows like *Boots and Saddles*, *Tales of Wells Fargo* and *Gunsmoke*.

One of Hollywood's best-known casting directors, Lynn Stallmaster, helped get Western on the popular CBS show *Have Gun, Will Travel* in March 1958 in an episode entitled "The Return of Doctor Thackery," co-starring June Lockhart, who later played Timmy's mom on the show *Lassie*. In the show, Western plays a young cowboy who challenges star Richard Boone (Paladin) to a gunfight in which he is quickly shot and wounded.

A Hollywood publicity shot of Johnny Western, 1963. Western wrote the popular theme song to the CBS television show *Have Gun, Will Travel*. It was a thank-you gift to the producers and star Richard Boone for casting Western in the show. It soon became the show's closing theme, and more than fifty people have recorded "The Ballad of Paladin." Western became part of the Phoenix Sound after Ray Odom began booking him in various area clubs in the early 1960s. *Courtesy of Johnny Western. All rights reserved.*

Grateful that he had a chance to act on this popular show, Western sat down and wrote "The Ballad of Paladin" in twenty minutes and presented the song to Richard Boone and producer Sam Rolfe as a musical thank-you. The next thing he knew, they were using the song as the show's theme; you could hear Johnny Western singing the ballad over the closing credits to each week's show. In the show's heyday, it ran in over seventy countries.

On the set of *Have Gun, Will Travel*, starring Richard Boone (far right) and Johnny Western (far left). This is a still shot from the episode where Western challenges Paladin to a gunfight, 1958. *Courtesy of Johnny Western. All rights reserved.*

Western said the song has been known as the "Johnny Western Annuity" and eventually was recorded by more than fifty people, including Duane Eddy, who had the highest-charting single of the song. The royalties continue to this day, more than fifty years later.

One day, Western said he almost drove off the Hollywood freeway after hearing a singer with a very unique style on the radio. Johnny Cash was riding the Sun Records rocket out of Memphis, rubbing shoulders with Jerry Lee Lewis and a cat named Elvis Presley. Western met Cash at a show in Canada and was hired to play guitar on three gigs with the "Man in Black."

Those performances turned into thirty-nine years of playing with Cash on the road and in studio work, recording seventy-one singles and playing on five Cash albums for Columbia Records. Some of the songs Western played guitar on include "The Rebel Johnny Yuma" and "Tennessee Flat-top Box." "I loved playing with Johnny Cash because he rarely took more than two or three takes when recording a song," said Western.

Western toured with Johnny Cash when he played his first show at San Quinten Prison in 1960. In the front row was a young prisoner named Merle Haggard. Haggard had become a trustee and managed to join the prison band. He was in the joint for attempted robbery of a Bakersfield business. Many years later, Western said he was playing the Blackboard nightclub in Bakersfield, and Haggard was playing in the house band making fifteen dollars a night and seventy-five dollars a week. "Haggard thought that was all the money in the world back then," recalled Western.

Johnny Cash and Western were such good friends that, according to Western, Cash extended to him an incredible act of kindness after a horrific car accident in Wyoming in 1976 as he was heading to the Cheyenne Frontier Days Rodeo. A band member who was driving fell asleep at the wheel and rolled the car at least fifteen times on Interstate 80 at five o'clock in the morning. A passing truck driver stopped and applied pressure to his wounds until medical help arrived. Western was laid up in the hospital for weeks. Cash called and told him not to worry about the medical bills, which totaled some $17,000. "I've arranged to have the bill sent to me," Cash said. "You just concentrate on getting well." Western said that Johnny Cash was a true life-long friend all the way to the end, when he passed in 2003.

Johnny Western became a big part of the Phoenix Sound and the local music scene when Ray Odom booked him at the Riverside Ballroom in 1960. Western got close with all the local players, including Duane Eddy and Waylon Jennings. Jennings booked him into J.D.'s nightclub in Tempe in 1966 just before he left for Nashville after signing with RCA Records. "Matter of fact, Waylon introduced me to my wife, Jo, at J.D.'s," Western said. To date, Johnny and Jo Western have been married for nearly fifty years.

In the '80s, musician Gary Clemmons became Johnny's band leader and, along with Ronnie Derrosett and Michael Hounshell, toured as his backup band known as the Arizona Rangers. Clemmons said Western was the consummate entertainer.

In 1986, Western went back to a radio career and spent twenty-five years at KFDI in Wichita, Kansas. His deal with the station allowed him to also play concerts throughout the year. Western has toured all over the world and even played on the Great Wall of China with singer Rex Allen Jr. and the Prairie Rose Wrangler Band.

Western is in twelve halls of fame, including the Country Disc Jockey Hall of Fame; in April 2015, he was inducted into the Arizona Music and Entertainment Hall of Fame. His song "The Ballad of Paladin" was voted the number one TV western theme song of all time by people's choice in *American Cowboy* magazine in its January 2015 issue.

After sixty-four years in show business, Johnny and Jo returned to retire in Mesa, Arizona, in 2010.

Dolan Ellis: Arizona State Balladeer

Growing up on the windswept Kansas plains, Dolan Ellis told me he felt a calling at a young age to move and live in Arizona. "I was always fascinated by the cowboy, Hispanic and western lifestyle," Ellis said. All through high school and at Kansas University, where he majored in journalism, his dream never faltered.

In 1959, he made that move, and it was a decision he never regretted. He became a part of the local Phoenix music scene and joined an international singing group that would take him around the world. To supplement his musical income, he worked as a TV cameraman at KOOL television Channel 10 when he first hit town. He began playing in the local folk music clubs. Folk music was hot at the time. Groups like the Kingston Trio were climbing the charts and drawing big crowds.

Ellis soon scored the big prize: a gig at the popular Portofino's Coffee House in Scottsdale. This afforded him the opportunity to open for big-name folk singers, including the Gateway Singers, Bud and Travis and others. Not long after, he opened his own club, called simply Dolan's. "I even hired a young John Denver to perform at my club before he hit the big time," said Ellis.

Soon, his fascination with Arizona became fodder for his music. He wrote songs about the history of the state, from its rich Native American and Hispanic influences to the free-spirit, cowboy-and-western lifestyle that remains the life blood of Arizona, not to mention the incredible landscapes from the desert to the mountains and beyond. Ellis is quick to tell you that Arizona is part of his soul.

In the early 1960s, musician Randy Sparks recruited Ellis to become a part of a big innovative folk vocal group he called the New Christy

A young Dolan Ellis dominated the Phoenix Sound within the local folk music scene. He also became a member of the New Christy Minstrels and won Grammy Awards and gold records with the group. The group was a regular on the weekly *Andy Williams* television show. Back in Arizona, Ellis opened his own nightclub, and in 1966, Arizona governor Sam Goddard named him the official Arizona state balladeer. *Courtesy of Dolan Ellis. All rights reserved.*

Minstrels. The group began selling out shows nationwide, singing songs such as "Green, Green," "This Land Is Your Land" and others. Soon, the group began appearing as regulars on the weekly *Andy Williams* television show and won Grammy Awards, gold records and worldwide fame.

Money and recognition are one thing, but in 1963, Ellis was missing Arizona and abruptly quit the group to go home. "People told me I was crazy," he said. "Why would I give up the fame and fortune and success the group was having? I stayed with the Minstrels through the first four albums. I just missed Arizona, and besides, I had bigger plans for my career."

Ellis set down roots in Scottsdale and along the way became pretty good friends with many of the other local entertainers who later made it big in the music business. "I was good friends with Waylon Jennings," he said. "We used to have breakfast almost every morning at the now-defunct Safari Hotel coffee shop after playing our respective nightclub gigs.

"One night Waylon comes in, and he is just glowing and grinning from ear to ear! I said, 'What's up?' Waylon says, 'Chet Atkins at RCA Records just signed me to a big recording contract!' Jennings said, 'I was wondering if it would be OK with you if I record that song you sing called "Four Strong Winds?"' I told Waylon I didn't write the song. Canadian songwriter Ian Tyson wrote it. You don't need my permission. Just register it with the publisher and make sure that Tyson gets credit as the songwriter. Jennings was very naïve in those days and was still learning how the music business operated," Ellis said. "'But would you write out the lyrics and chords for me?' Jennings asked. So I wrote out the lyrics and chord progressions out on the back of a paper restaurant placemat. Next thing I know is I am driving down the street one day and hear Jennings singing 'Four Strong Winds' on the radio, as he had recorded it, and it was one of his first releases. I was proud and pleased that I indirectly helped old Waylon chart one of his first songs in country music."

In 1966, Arizona governor Sam Goddard named Dolan Ellis the official Arizona state balladeer. He was the first state balladeer in the nation. Since then, a number of states have followed suit. Every governor since then has reappointed him. In 2016, Ellis celebrated fifty years in that position.

Ellis also pioneered the use of video technology in his stage shows. "I think I was the first in the nation, as I started doing it about six months after the equipment was invented," he said. The visual images of Arizona just add to the flavor of the music. Ellis and a partner, Lance Bellville, also wrote a western musical called *Cowgirls*. It was an all-girl cast and toured some fifty cities nationwide.

"In 1985, I reached a point I wanted to do more than just shows night after night. I wanted to leave behind something more significant. I wanted to build a Southwest Folklore and Cultural Center," Ellis stated. "We found this beautiful place in Ramsey Canyon, south of Sierra Vista." There, Ellis put together a 501(c)3 nonprofit and partnered up with the University of Arizona to finally get it built. Ellis is the monthly artist in residence. He and other singers perform there regularly.

Dolan Ellis still performs to appreciative audiences and will celebrate fifty years as the official state balladeer of Arizona in 2016. He is also the artist in residence at the Arizona Folklore Preserve near Sierra Vista, Arizona. *Courtesy of Dolan Ellis. All rights reserved.*

Like many an entertainer, Ellis spends days and weeks on the road traveling from gig to gig. "The road will just wear and tear you down. The constant travel, bad eating habits, long hours away from home, jet lag and not sleeping well will all take their toll," he said. "Whenever I got home from being on the road for any length of time, it would take me the better part of a week to function properly again. I would be just drained."

In 2015, Ellis toured with a newly re-formed New Christy Minstrels: "We toured with six of the original eight members for a while. It was very special."

Ellis also marvels at the incredible number of talented people who have come out of Phoenix and Arizona. "Phoenix was just a little burg back in those years and to have so much talent come out of this dusty middle-of-the-desert town is pretty amazing," he said.

But Dolan Ellis is just a little concerned about who is going to fill his shoes when he is gone. "Though it's really not my decision on who will be the next state balladeer, I have a few people in mind that might be able to carry on this tradition," he said. "Hopefully someday soon someone will step up to carry the torch to a new generation and speak and sing about a special place called Arizona!"

OTHER PICKERS, GRINNERS, ROCKABILLY SINGERS AND MORE

Many local musicians and talent were on the edge of the big time. Many were content to play local venues and shows, but others who recorded at the Audio Recorders, VIV or Porter Sound studios in Phoenix were hoping for that one big record. Along the way, there were a few successful songwriters who wrote big hit records for others. You might not know their names, but you would recognize their hit songs. Here are even more of the Phoenix Sound players.

Virg Warner

Virg Warner was a local Phoenix-area singer who played the nightclub circuit in the Phoenix valley. Warner told me in an interview that he got into the local music scene while attending Phoenix College, where he met singer Donnie Owens. It wasn't long after that he met businessman Bob Sikora, who was about to open up the huge Mr. Lucky's nightclub off Grand Avenue and Indian School Roads on the west side of town.

Mr. Sikora hired Warner and his band, the Rogues, and they played the popular Mr. Lucky's club from 1966 to 1978. The pickers in his band were all seasoned pros, including Billy Williams on lead guitar, Stan Oscarson on bass guitar and Terry Wells on drums. Terry would end up moving to Nashville, where he would play drums for Grand Ole Opry singer Dottie

West for several years before she was killed in an automobile accident. Warner also worked with longtime area drummer Ron Corbin. In 1972, J. David Sloan joined the Rogues Band. He took over as lead singer when Warner left the band in 1978.

Warner cut a few demos at Audio Recorders of songs written by Dale Noe and others and then ended up becoming friends with producer Lee Hazlewood. He was the first to record on Hazlewood's new label, LHI. He recorded nine singles on the LHI label, and five of them charted.

Capitol Records A&R man Joe Allison signed Warner to the label, and one of the first songs he recorded was his version of "Sing a Sad Song," written by Wynn Stewart and an early hit for Merle Haggard.

Warner continued to write his own songs and for a time went on the road with singer Marty Mitchell and Ron Corbin. "We were known as the Wild Honey Trio," said Warner. "We even changed our name from time to time." In fact, he and Mitchell are still writing music and keeping their hands in the music business today.

Virg Warner moved to Nashville and was a songwriter there for twenty years. He wrote "I Still Love You in the Same Old Way," which was a top-fifteen hit for country singer Moe Bandy. Bandy recorded other songs that Warner penned. Warner also had a couple songs he wrote recorded by Merle Haggard and Jack Greene. Having moving back out west in 1998, Virg Warner lives in the city of Prescott, Arizona, today.

Donnie Owens

Local singer Donnie Owens (no relation to Buck Owens) and the 4 Jacks played for almost five years at a nightclub called Harry's Capri Lounge. Owens was a popular local musician and reliable go-to session guitarist on a variety of sessions at the local studios. In 1958, Owens had a minor hit nationally with a Buddy Wheeler–written tune called "Need You." He recorded it at the local VIV recording studio. It would reach number twenty-five on the *Billboard* Hot 100 chart. Duane Eddy played acoustic guitar on the session. Owens even appeared on Dick Clark's *American Bandstand* to promote the song. Tragically, Donnie Owens was accidently killed by a girlfriend in 1994.

Buddy Long

Buddy Long was a very important player in a group called the Sunset Riders. This was the group that played on Ray Odom's Arizona Hayride shows every Saturday at the Madison Square Garden club in the mid-1950s. Al Casey, Duane Eddy, Jimmy Dell and Buddy Wheeler were all members of the band, among others. In the '60s, Paul "Buddy" Long continued to be a popular draw wherever he played. Not long after Waylon Jennings hit town, Long recorded a song called "River Boy," on which Jennings played lead guitar. Buddy Long and the River Boys backed up many national touring acts. The band played at many different clubs, including a place called R.G.'s near Tempe and Mesa, Arizona. Bo Tucker would bring his young ten-year-old daughter, Tanya, to the club for jam sessions on Sunday afternoons.

Stand-out tunes that Buddy Long recorded include a 1966 tune produced by Jennings and recorded at Audio Recorders called "Walk My Loneliness Home" and "It's Nothin' to Me." He also recorded several other country songs. According to longtime Arizona musician Gary Clemmons, "Buddy worked hard to gain as much local and regional success as he could. He went on to work with Jennings at the river bottom club called J.D.'s with Richie Albright on drums and Jerry Gropp on guitar, and Waylon dubbed them his 'Waylors.' After Jennings signed on with RCA Records in Nashville, Long went on the road on tour for several months."

Buddy Long remained based in Phoenix but would go off on six-month-long tours of Alaska when they were building the big oil pipeline, making big money in local clubs. He'd work the Mint Hotel in Reno for extended runs. Long continued to be a popular draw for years. In later years, Buddy Long lived in the small town of Dewey, just outside Prescott, Arizona, where he passed away in June 2008.

Ray Sharpe

Hailing from Fort Worth, Texas, Ray Sharpe had a minor couple of hits that charted on DOT Records. Lee Hazlewood produced his first session at Ramsey's studio in 1958. Sharpe had success on the music charts with the song "Linda Lu" on the Jamie label. It reached number forty-six on *Billboard* in 1959 with Hazlewood producing, Duane Eddy on lead and Al Casey on rhythm guitar. Sharpe was an accomplished lead and blues guitarist, but Hazlewood wanted Eddy on lead guitar on "Linda Lu." Sharpe charted several other songs on the Jamie label, but none was a big hit.

Chuck Mayfield

Mayfield hailed from Fort Smith, Arkansas. As a young man, he signed a record deal with Starday Records out of Nashville in 1952. He also had deals with Abbott Records and DOT Records at some point. He was invited to join the KWKH Louisiana Hayride and was a popular fixture on the WFAA *Dallas Shindig* and the *Houston Jamboree* radio shows. Migrating to Arizona, he wound up working at KCKY Radio in Coolidge doing a fifteen-minute radio show in 1956. Ray Odom soon signed him to the Saturday night Arizona Hayride show at the Phoenix Garden. He developed such a following that people started to refer to him as "the Eloy Flash."

Ritchie Hart

Charles "Ritchie" Gearhart began life in small Goose Creek, Kentucky, and settled in Phoenix when his family moved while he was still a student in high school. Managing to grab a gig at Audio Recorders, he charted a song called "The Great Duane," backed with "I'm Hypnotised," on the tiny Felstead label in 1959. Shortening his name to Hart, he recorded for Ramsey's Ramco and MCI labels, and his band became Ritchie Hart and the Hartbeats. In the late '60s, Hart helped form the group Goose Creek Symphony, and the band signed with Capitol Records in Hollywood. The group has also been inducted into the Arizona Music and Entertainment Hall of Fame.

Alvie Self

A genuine Arizona-born and bred singer who once upon a time was a rodeo cowboy, Alvie Self has been singing and performing since the 1950s. He scored a bona fide rockabilly hit with a song called "Let's Go Wild," backed

Alvie Self was a cowboy from Cottonwood, Arizona, who recorded a few rockabilly singles in Phoenix; they were released on the Don-Ray label. One of his best was "Let's Go Wild." He still performs today at resort hotels and ranches in Arizona. *Courtesy of Alvie Self. All rights reserved.*

with "Nancy," on the DonRay label. Alvie started out playing an accordion but switched to a solid-body Les Paul guitar and Magnatone amp. Recording at Loy Clingman's VIV studio in Phoenix, his first single, "Rain Dance," was on the Ford label. Phoenix and Los Angeles studio legend Al Casey played piano on the single "I See Your Love."

Born in Cottonwood, Arizona, Self still performs today, and his shows at the M-Diamond dude ranch are memorable to many out-of-state visitors.

Bob Cox

Bob Cox was a popular singer and musician in the Prescott, Arizona area for many, many years. Other budding musicians would seek out Cox to teach them how to be better pickers and players. He was a good and well-respected musician and an even better man.

Growing up in Sweetwater, Texas, in 1939, Cox settled near Glendale-Peoria, Arizona, and began working farm labor and performing. Poor eyesight

Bob Cox was a popular country singer in the Prescott, Arizona area who early on performed with many other local singers, including Marty Robbins and Alvie Self. *Left to right*: Bob Cox and Rod Hart. *Courtesy of Tina Cox-Clemmons.*

kept him out of the navy in World War II, but Cox did his part to entertain the troops at the nearby Veterans Hospital at Fort Whipple, near Prescott.

In the 1940s and '50s, Cox performed on local radio with such newcomers as Marty Robbins in several talent contests and also played with Jimmy Wakely and Dub Taylor. He even had his own label, Magnet Records. Signing with producer Fabor Robison, who was producing and recording several acts, including Jim Reeves, Cox had many opportunities to go on the road but decided to stay put in Prescott to raise his family. He played in the many bars and watering holes along Prescott's famous Whiskey Row, including the historic Palace Saloon.

The decision not to travel far prevented Cox from achieving any bigger success. Despite that decision, he did have regional radio hits such as "If You'll Be Mine Again," which made it to number one on Phoenix KHAT Radio. The song "Don't Hold Her So Close" hit the top ten in Phoenix and was number one on a station in Alaska.

In 1971, the movie *Junior Bonner*, starring Steve McQueen, was shot in and around Prescott, including at the Palace bar on Whiskey Row. The movie's producers hired Bob Cox and his local house band after hearing how good they sounded. The song "Arizona Morning" was co-written by Cox and singer-songwriter Rod Hart and was supposed to be featured in the opening credits of *Junior Bonner*, but a conflict and personal falling out with Hart—which was later reconciled—led to that song being pulled from the movie.

Jeb Rosebrook, an Arizona resident who wrote the screenplay for *Junior Bonner*, said, "The song 'Arizona Morning' was included in the original opening of the film. ABC Pictures, now owned by Disney, bought the rights to 'Morning' and later replaced it with a song by Livingston Taylor, who originally was supposed to have a song in the film. So 'Arizona Morning' is only in the original VHS version of the movie and not on later DVD versions."

One day in 2013, a Cox family member was watching a cable TV show called *Justified*. In the background of a scene, a song was playing. It was "Drifting Home to You." "We immediately knew it was one of Daddy's songs," said Tina Cox-Clemmons. The producers of the show agreed to pay the surviving family members royalties on their late father's music used in the cable TV show.

Bob Cox lent a helping hand to many a struggling musician over the years. Many family and friends would like to see him inducted into the Arizona Music and Entertainment Hall of Fame for his contributions to Arizona music. Bob Cox passed away in the Prescott area in 2012.

Don Rollins

Don Rollins is probably another name you don't know. This singer-songwriter scored big with several songs that became country music standards. Rollins hung around the Phoenix studios. Back in the '60s, he recorded several songs at Loy Clingmans VIV studio, including "If I'm Wrong," which local singer Donnie Owens recorded on the flip side of his top-twenty-five song "Need You." Rollins even recorded on Lee Hazlewood's LHI records. According to the *VIV Story* liner notes on the Bear Family Records label, Rollins met Buck Owens's sister Dorothy in 1961 and ended up sending Buck several songs he'd written, including a demo called "Mirror Mirror." Owens changed some of the lyric for half the writer's credits and recorded the song as "Mirror, Mirror on the Wall." The song appears on Owens's 1962 Capitol album *You're for Me*. Rollins also wrote a major country hit for singer Ray Price and penned "The Race Is On," which George Jones took to the stratosphere in 1964.

Local singer Jimmy Grey reportedly cut the first demo of the song, and even Waylon Jennings recorded it on the one and only A&M Records album he recorded for Herb Alpert and Jerry Moss. Today, "The Race Is On" is a bona fide country music standard recorded by many other acts, including Sawyer Brown, the Grateful Dead, Travis Tritt, Jack Jones and even the Chipmunks. Rollins's inspiration to write it reportedly came after visiting the legendary Turf Paradise horse-racing track in Phoenix, which has been open since the early 1950s.

Not long after, Rollins pitched the song "The Other Woman (in My Life)" to singer Ray Price, who added it to his stable of great country hits, and it was published by Pamper Music in Nashville. Sadly, after four years of writing songs, Rollins never had any other hits, and he took his own life on June 28, 1968—an incredibly sad ending for such a bright young writer and musician who not only contributed mightily to the Phoenix Sound but also wrote songs that have become country music standards.

Dale Noe

Like I mentioned in previous chapters, there were so many talented singers and songwriters who contributed to the music scene in Arizona and nationwide. Dale Noe would gain some national fame as the composer of several songs that went on to be country music classics. Noe

Local Phoenix songwriter Dale Noe would write several big hits for various artists such as Jim Reeves and wrote the number-one song "It's Such a Pretty World Today" for West Coast singer Wynn Stewart. It was Stewart's only number-one hit. *Courtesy of Gary Davis.*

wrote "Missing You," "Missing Angel" and "Angels Don't Lie" for velvet-voiced singer Jim Reeves. "Missing You" was recorded at Reeves's very last RCA session in Nashville prior to the tragic light plane crash that took his life in 1964. The song was released as a single in 1972 by Reeves's widow, Mary Reeves-Davis. It hit the top ten on the *Billboard* country charts. "Angels Don't Lie" would chart as a top-five hit. But Dale Noe is best known as the songwriter of "It's Such a Pretty World Today" for West Coast–based singer Wynn Stewart. It became Stewart's only number-one record in 1967 and was song of the year and nominated for a Grammy Award.

Years later, Noe wrote the song "After the Storm," which was poised to be a big comeback hit for Wynn Stewart, who had been off the charts for several years. Unfortunately, while preparing for the big tour to promote the song, Wynn Stewart died of a heart attack.

Dale Noe was originally from Ohio but fronted many bands from El Paso to Phoenix for many years. Our paths crossed a few times while I worked in country radio. I remember him as a pleasant, good-natured man. Noe died in Phoenix in November 2004.

George Richey

Back in about 1959, George Richey was working as a radio DJ at country KMOP in Tucson, Arizona, which was partly owned by media mogul Ray Odom. That same year, he recorded a rockabilly song at Ramsey's studio called "Not in a Million Years" on the Smart Record label. By the mid-'60s, he was a producer in a small studio in Tucson and began writing songs. Later, he moved Nashville and continued songwriting; he wrote or co-wrote songs like "A Picture of Me without You" and "The Grand Tour" for George Jones, plus several songs for Tammy Wynette, including "Till I Can Make It on My Own." Richey married Wynette in the late '70s and became her manager until her death in 1998.

Ted Newman

"I sort of backed into the music business by accident," said Ted Newman. "One day, I get a call from Jack Miller, the engineer at Audio Recorders in

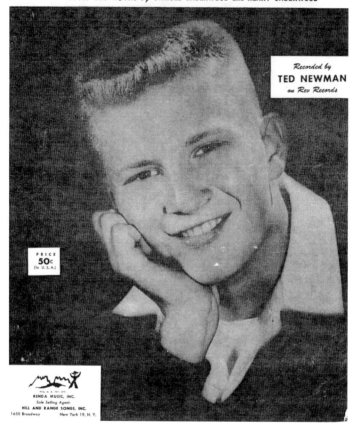

Local singer Ted Newman scored a top-forty-five hit with "Plaything" in 1958, another national success story that was part of the Phoenix Sound. Newman still writes songs and performs today. *Courtesy of Ted Newman. All rights reserved.*

Phoenix. Miller told me that they were looking for a singer to record a couple of tracks at the studio, and was I interested?" Newman had recorded some local commercial jingles, and Miller was familiar with his work.

"The song was called 'Plaything,'" said Newman, "and the day we recorded it there was a who's who of local pickers in the studio, including Connie Conway, who was also an A&R man; Jimmy Wilcox, along with producer Floyd Ramsey; and Jack Miller, who engineered. We recorded 'Plaything' in the spring of 1957." Within a few short weeks, it started climbing the *Billboard* music chart and stopped at number forty-five nationwide.

"All of a sudden, I find myself hanging out with Dick Clark on *American Bandstand*. I appeared twice on the show in 1957," said Newman. "Plaything" came several months after the chart success of "The Fool" by Sanford Clark—yet another successful song that had been recorded in Phoenix. "Soon, I ended up on a ten-day promotional tour of the East Coast in places like Philadelphia; Wilmington, Delaware; then back to the Midwest and Chicago," Newman recalled.

In those days, it was a fairly common practice for several singers to record the same song and release their versions around the same time to try to take advantage of the song's momentum. One example is singer Guy Mitchell, who recorded a pop version of the song "Singin' the Blues" about the same time as Marty Robbins's version was climbing the country charts. Mitchell's version sort of stole some of the thunder of the Robbins recording.

The same thing happened to Ted Newman. A young man named Nick Todd also recorded his version of "Plaything." Todd was Pat Boone's younger brother, so while Newman had the bigger hit with the song, Todd's version sort of watered down the impact of Newman's record even though it was released on Randy Wood's DOT Records, which had pretty good nationwide distribution, exposure and radio airplay. Within three or four months, the song was over on the charts.

Newman had a few other minor hits and is still writing songs today. You can still find him performing in Arizona and Colorado. In 2012, during Arizona's centennial celebration, Newman was named one of one hundred Arizona Culture Keepers. That in itself is quite an honor.

Loy Clingman

Loy was a fixture in the local Phoenix Sound for many years, including as part owner of VIV Records and recording studio, which competed with Ramseys-Audio Recorders. Clingman was a local schoolteacher who dabbled in the music business and produced many fine country and rockabilly recordings, including the Leon Payne song "Its Nothin' to Me" and "Rockin Down Mexico Way," which had Duane Eddy and Wayne Newton, along with Wayne's brother Jerry, performing on the session. Mr. Clingman died in 2011.

Jimmy Spellman

Born in Ohio, Jimmy Spellman and his family moved to Phoenix in 1954, and for several years the family uprooted young Jimmy from school in Arizona and moved back and forth from Ohio to Phoenix. According to historian John P. Dixon and writer Johnny Vallis, Spellman said, "The first week I arrived in Phoenix, I auditioned for the local *Lew King Rangers* kiddie show along with Wayne and Jerry Newton, who had also moved to Phoenix for Wayne's asthma condition. Wayne, Jerry and I performed on the show for quite some time."

Spellman recorded on the VIV label, among others, and his first release was "No Need to Cry Anymore" in September 1955. His style was described as a little pop, a little country, and had a sound and feel similar to Ricky Nelson's. Spellman would build quite a following in Arizona. Promoter Ray Odom had hired Spellman as a regular on the Saturday night Arizona Hayride show at Madison Square Garden. Not only did Odom keep Spellman busy on the stage show and TV show, but he also booked him on a nationwide Grand Ole Opry package show; he also traveled with big stars at the time like Faron Young, Webb Pierce, Brenda Lee, Marty Robbins, Wanda Jackson, Porter Wagoner and others. It was a grueling schedule that had him performing nearly every night of the week, twice on Saturdays. He had Sundays off.

Bear Family Records out of Germany has produced an extensive compilation CD of Spellman's career called *Doggonit* and mentions that Spellman not only recorded for the VIV label but also for DOT and several other imprints, including VIK, REV and Redstart. Some songs were leased to RCA Records. In 1960, he was recording with the cream of the local pickers and session men, including Al Casey, Jimmy Wilcox, Connie Conway, Bob Taylor, Jimmy Johnson, Forrest Skaggs and, of course, Jack Miller in master control at Audio Recorders.

In those liner notes by Jack Vallis, one DOT Records session shows just what a taskmaster and perfectionist Lee Hazlewood was while producing Spellman. "The Second DOT session and the song 'I'll Never Smile Again' took 144 takes! Although the backing track was complete, except for Al Casey's guitar work, I was exhausted and thought I'd never smile again!" Spellman said.

By the mid-1960s, Jimmy Spellman had quit recording to raise a family; he worked for Motorola and, later, the City of Phoenix. He told me he retired from the city in 2005 and has no regrets today. He is humble, though, about the fact that he contributed to the success of the Phoenix Sound.

Jimmy Spellman had several hits on the local Phoenix labels, as well as DOT Records nationally. He was a popular performer, and Ray Odom booked him regularly on the Arizona Hayride show on Saturday nights at the Madison Square Garden club. Spellman is retired and living in Phoenix today. *Courtesy of John P. Dixon. All rights reserved.*

Gary LeMel

Originally from England, Gary LeMel grew up in Tucson, Arizona, and was once a member of the famous Tucson Boys Choir and had his own local TV show. In 1958, he came up to Phoenix to record for the REV label at Audio Recorders. He recorded a high-energy rockabilly tune called "Rockin' in the Halls." He even appeared on *American Bandstand* with Dick Clark but failed to score a big hit with the song.

After a stint in the army in Vietnam, LeMel signed with VeeJay Records in 1964 and had a modest hit. He is best known for being a record music executive on several major labels and has worked in artist management for Jerry Weintraub. He's also known for supervising the production of many award-winning movie soundtracks, such as *A Star Is Born*, *Ghostbusters*, *The Big Chill*, *The Bodyguard* and others. He is also an accomplished jazz musician.

Skip and Flip

In 1958, the duo of Skip and Flip recorded a song at Ramsey's studio that would become a million-selling record with "It Was I." Skip and Flip consisted of songwriter Gary S. Paxton as "Skip" and Clyde Batten as "Flip." They met as college students at the University of Arizona in Tucson. The songs "It Was I" and "Cherry Pie" would garner big airplay on the Chart label.

Gary and Clyde would also record under the name The Pledges and cut a song called "Betty Jean" on the REV label in 1958.

Gary S. Paxton would go on to other music success and is partially responsible for the number-one novelty songs "The Monster Mash" with Bobby "Boris" Pickett and "Alley Oop" by the Hollywood Argyles, the latter written by Dallas Frazier, who wrote a ton of classic country songs during his career. Paxton dabbled in country music for a time and has written and recorded award-winning gospel songs. He has been labeled an eccentric, creative and over-the-top workaholic but tirelessly continues in the music business to this day. Clyde Batten reportedly moved on to join the band The Byrds with Roger McQuinn.

Howard Roberts

You have heard this man's guitar playing whether you know it or not. His music has been featured on many, many television shows, including *The Twilight Zone*; *Bonanza*; *The Munsters*; *Wild, Wild West*; *Batman*; *The Beverly Hillbillies*; and countless others. In addition, this guitarist has a connection to many of the Phoenix Sound musicians, as he played on many local sessions. He was also an accomplished jazz guitarist.

Howard Roberts was born in Phoenix in October 1929. He started playing guitar at age eight and was touring by the time he was sixteen. In 1950, Roberts moved to Los Angeles, where he hooked up with musicians Bobby Troup ("Get Your Kicks on Route 66") and Barney Kessel. Troup helped him get signed to Verve Records as a solo act. He moved into the role of a studio session player as well. He would become part of the famous "Wrecking Crew" of Los Angeles session musicians and worked alongside other great talents like Al Casey, Glen Campbell and several others.

In the late 1950s and into the '60s, he also backed up many Phoenix-area acts, such as Duane Eddy and singer and actor Johnny Western. "Howard Roberts played on the very first session I did for Columbia Records when we did the first version of 'The Ballad of Paladin,'" Western said. That session was recorded in Hollywood at Radio Recorders studio.

In later years, Roberts wrote a column for *Guitar Player* magazine and taught lessons. He died of prostate cancer at the young age of sixty-two in 1992. His music and teachings still influence musicians today. The late Don Rich, lead guitar player of Buck Owens and the Buckaroos fame, was reportedly a fan of Roberts's guitar stylings.

Curtis Lee

Curtis Lee was another performer who was not an actual part of the Phoenix music scene but came close. The Yuma, Arizona–born singer struck chart gold in 1961 with "Pretty Little Angel Eyes." The doo-wop-type song was his biggest hit, reaching number seven on the *Billboard* music charts.

After being discovered in a Tucson nightclub, Lee met songwriters Tommy Boyce and Bobby Hart, and the three wrote "Angel Eyes." He recorded the song on the West Coast with producer Phil Spector. Lee soon would be touring with Jerry Lee Lewis, Ricky Nelson and other acts of the day. His music career was a short one, though, and he had only one other single, a top-fifty song called "Under the Moon of Love."

After that, the hits dried up, and he went to work with his father in the construction industry in Yuma. According to the *Yuma Sun* newspaper, Lee told an oldies radio station that his biggest disappointment was not getting all of the music royalties due to him. He passed away in January 2015 at age seventy-five. Lee was involved in many community events and was well liked in his hometown.

Jimmy Patton

Born in Oklahoma in 1931, Jimmy Patton dabbled in rock-and-roll and country music on the West Coast in the mid-'50s. He recorded songs like "Yeah, I'm Movin" and "Let Me Slide." In about 1960, he recorded "Okies in the Pokie" at Audio Recorders. It was probably his biggest and bestselling hit. Donnie Owens reportedly played guitar on the session. In later years, Patton released a country album recorded in Bakersfield. He died after a drunk driver slammed into his car in Oregon in 1989.

Billy Barnett

In the year 1955, Billy Barnett was known as a regional country music singer, according to historian John P. Dixon. He mainly played around the state of Arizona with Billy Hughes, another contemporary. Together they recorded "Romp and Stomp" at Ramsey's studio in Phoenix and pressed the song on the tiny Double-D label out of Wickenburg, Arizona. It was backed by Keith Kolby and the Desert Suns.

Billy Hughes and the Rhythm Buckaroos

Mr. Hughes left his mark early in country music circles. Born in Oklahoma in 1908, Everette-Ishmael "Billy" Hughes wrote a few hit songs and helped many an aspiring artists get started. He wrote the number-one song

"Tennessee Saturday Night" for Grand Ole Opry singer Red Foley and also wrote songs for Eddy Arnold and Spade Cooley. In addition, he worked with Ernest Tubb and Tex Williams.

In the late 1930s, after living in California, he migrated to Arizona for a time to play with singers like Bob Cox out of Prescott and Billy Barnett. Billy Hughes passed away in 1995.

Joe Montgomery

With titles like "Cool Cat," "The Bowling Song" and "Planetary Run," Joe Montgomery was living in Tucson in the late 1950s when he came up to Phoenix to the Ramsey studio and recorded for Liberty Bell and Abbott Records. Historian John P. Dixon told me that Jamie Records had passed on "Planetary Run." Al Casey played the amped-up guitar on that session, and that could have been a big record for Montgomery. We will never know.

Don Cole

Another versatile musician was Don Cole, who seemed to live in the Ramsey studio and played various gigs around the Phoenix valley. If Al Casey wasn't available, Cole could fill in with just as good guitar riffs on various sessions. Among the songs he recorded was one called "Stop" at the Porter Sound studio in 1958. Don Cole died in Phoenix in 1977.

Bob "Easy Deal" Wilson

From what I understand and researched, Bob "Easy Deal" Wilson was quite a character around Phoenix. He was born in Dallas, Texas, but never lived there, apparently. He migrated to the Southwest doing a variety of low-wage jobs before landing in Phoenix. He taught himself how to play piano and went to what was then Arizona State College on a football scholarship and, according to Wilson, majored in meeting girls.

At one point, he owned a bar called Easy Deals. Wilson recorded the song "Gotta Have You" and, later, a novelty song called "Ain't No Freckles on My Fish." Loy Clingman signed him to the VIV label. "Neither one did much nationally, but I got a shitload of local radio airplay," Wilson was quoted as saying.

Frank Fafara

Frank Fafara was a teen heartthrob in Phoenix and a popular pop and rock singer in the area. He attended Brophy High School. In 1959, he recorded "Only in My Dreams," which became a hit locally at KRIZ Radio, where it landed in the top ten at number five on the local radio chart. *Cashbox* magazine said, "Fafara has something of the Buddy Holly in his light beat delivery."

"I used to play early on at the downtown Phoenix Fox Theater with Wayne Newton and his brother Jerry," said Fafara. That was one of his first performances. Frank's band consisted of Richard Meyer on lead guitar, Jim Shultz on drums and Fafara on rhythm. Al Casey played bass on some of his cuts. It was all recorded with Jack Miller engineering at Audio Recorders. They were pleasantly surprised when their first single, "Only in My Dreams," turned out so well. That first single was with MCI Records.

Fafara began performing on a TV show called *Teen Beat*, which was hosted by local Phoenix media icon Pat McMahon on KPHO Channel 5. Local musician Mike Condello performed on the show as well. They played gigs all over the state

Other songs Fafara recorded include "The Golden One" and "Lovemaker, Lovebreaker." Fafara signed with local promoter Jack Curtis at Mascot Records and played at a popular teen nightclub called Stage 7 on Seventh Street, just north of Indian School Road. He was also a semi-regular on the wildly popular *Wallace and Ladmo* children's show in Phoenix.

Frank Fafara and his wife, Patty Parker, live in Fountain Hills, Arizona. Together they run Comstock Records. They market country music to audiences worldwide. Besides owning a thriving music business, they also market Fafara's music, and that of others, to movies and television shows such as *The Good Wife*.

Right: Frank Fafara was a hugely popular rock-and-roll singer in Phoenix in the late 1950s to early '60s. He recorded for the local Mascot label. *Courtesy of Frank Fafara and Patty Parker. All rights reserved.*

Below: Frank Fafara on *Teen Beat*, a local teen show on Channel 5 in Phoenix hosted by local media icon Pat McMahon. *From left to right*: Fafara, singer-performer Mike Condello and Pat McMahon. *Courtesy of Frank Fafara and Patty Parker. All rights reserved.*

Mike Condello

Another talented musician and performer was Mike Condello. He recorded on Jack Curtis's Mascot Records and was a popular Phoenix-area singer. Condello was featured with Pat McMahon, Bill Thompson and Lad Kwiatkowski on the groundbreaking and long-running Phoenix children's TV show *Wallace and Ladmo*.

Condello was part of Hub-Cap and the Wheels, which earned a Capitol Records recording contract for a brief moment; he also fronted the Commodore Condello and the Salt River Navy Band. In addition, Condello and his band played basement gigs at the sprawling J.D.'s nightclub in Tempe, Arizona, when Waylon Jennings brought in country music crowds in the upstairs lounge.

Marty Mitchell

Marty Mitchell knew what he wanted to do at an early age, and that was sing and perform. He started at the age of twelve. When he was fourteen, the legendary Marty Robbins discovered him and invited the young Mitchell to perform with him on the Grand Ole Opry stage in Nashville. His career began to skyrocket in the next few years.

Marty was born in Birmingham, Alabama, and made the move to Arizona when he was sixteen. There he quickly made his mark on the Arizona music scene. Atlantic Records signed him to a deal at age seventeen, and the Motown Country label had tapped his talent by the time he was twenty-two. Music icons Berry Gordy and Mike Curb signed him, and with them his bluegrass version of "You Are the Sunshine of My Life" broke into the top forty on country charts.

Back home in Arizona, Mitchell kept busy with performances. Early on he performed in Virg Warner's band. He formed Marty Mitchell and Young Country, then the Arizona Band and finally the ever-popular Stumpwater Jak band, which included members Gary Clemmons, Michael Hounshell, Ronnie Derossett and Jerry Gropp, who had played with Waylon Jennings for several years. When Gropp passed away, Marty took his place in the popular group, which even charted a song, "Too Many Outlaws," on KNIX Radio in Phoenix.

Subsequent bands would include Smoke N Guns, which toured extensively in the Southwest. Marty left Arizona for a time to be a staff songwriter at several publishing houses in Nashville and has won a boatload of awards, including a Phoenix and Los Angeles Music Award. Marty Mitchell and I have been friends for a few years now, and I humbly admit that when the Phoenix Music Awards honored Marty with his award in 2008, they also gave me a plaque that same night for contributions to Phoenix radio over the years. That was very special.

Marty Mitchell has been an important player in the Phoenix music scene for the past forty years and continues to perform and amaze audiences today.

J. David Sloan, Ray Herndon and Buddy Alan Owens

Three musicians who certainly had an impact not only in Arizona but also nationally were J. David Sloan, Ray Herndon and Buddy Alan Owens. J. David was playing music when he was a young man and toured with many acts, including Willie Nelson. In about 1972, he was tiring of the music business and decided to relocate to Arizona and get into the construction industry. With musical friends in Phoenix, he was soon lured into fronting the Rogues Band after Virg Warner decided to move on. For over thirty years, Sloan was the bandleader at the very popular Mr. Lucky's club in Phoenix.

Through the years, J. David and the Rogues packed the house weekly. He showcased a lot of talent, including young Denise Conley and American Idol winner Jordin Sparks, who competed in talent contests and won many. Sloan also featured Lisa Martine. Her brother Reynaldo was an incredible guitar player who would wow the crowds. Lisa ended up in Nashville, where she was big with the Nashville musicians' union and the music licensing firm ASCAP. Other performers at Mr. Lucky's included Bill Hallock and Cactus County and Dal Perkins.

At one point, Sloan purchased the Mr. Lucky's nightclub from businessman Bob Sikora, and it remained a fixture in the city until it finally closed in 2004.

Sloan and members of the Rogues Band also recorded early sessions with Lyle Lovett and toured with Lovett around the country and the world. It all started in Phoenix.

Ray Herndon comes from a musical family. His brothers Ron and Rick formed a band called The Gringos when they were just kids growing up in Phoenix. Their father, Brick Herndon, was a popular guitar player and performer who went way back in the city's music history. Brick Herndon played with everybody from Marty Robbins to Bob Fite and His Western Playboys. Brick and his wife, Gwen, purchased a nightclub called Wild Bill's way up in the desert, north of Scottsdale, and renamed the place Handlebar J. For years, the family band performed at this club, and it still does today. The club is a must-visit venue for out-of-town folks looking for some great authentic country music.

Ray Herndon also played in the Rogues Band at Mr. Lucky's with J. David Sloan for a time, and in the 1990s, he became a member of the country trio McBride and the Ride out of Nashville. The group scored several big chart hits and a number-one record. Ray Herndon is one of the original musicians who helped launch Lyle Lovett's storied career and still tours with Lovett and his Large Band today.

The eldest son of country music legend Buck Owens, Buddy Alan Owens has made his mark in the music industry, too. While attending Arizona State University, he began recording and touring under the name Buddy Alan with his famous father in the late 1960s and into the early '70s. He charted many songs with Capitol Records; his best-known were "Big Mama's Medicine Show" and "Cowboy Convention," recorded with the late Don Rich. Buddy Alan also scored a number-seven hit, "Let the World Keep on A-Turnin'" with his father, Buck.

For many years, Buddy Alan performed with the Buckaroos band on the television show *Hee Haw*. Today, he occasionally performs at his late father's nightclub and museum, the Crystal Palace, in Bakersfield, California.

Honorable Mention: Stan Jones

The town of Douglas, Arizona, in the southeast part of the state near the historic copper mining town of Bisbee, lies along the Mexican border. Stan Jones was born and raised here with a huge southwestern influence. Jones's father actually knew the legendary bigger-than-life western icons Wyatt Earp and Doc Holliday from nearby Tombstone.

As a young boy, Jones was securing an old windmill from an approaching thunderstorm in the desert just outside his ranch house when an old cowhand named Cap Waits told him to look up at the sky and see the storm cloud formations that looked like "red eyed cows a-snortin'." The cowhand said they were the "devil's herd," according to an old Indian legend. Using his imagination, Jones could see that herd up in the sky.

In 1948, Jones became a park ranger for eighty dollars a month in one of the hottest places on earth, Death Valley, California, where temperatures can exceed 130 degrees in the summertime. On his thirty-fourth birthday, he looked up in the sky and saw those familiar storm clouds on the horizon and remembered that encounter he'd had with the old ranch hand years before. Inspiration struck, and he sat down and wrote a song called "Ghost Riders in the Sky." Actor and songwriter Johnny Western was a good friend of Stan Jones, and he tells me, "Stan went to Hollywood and actually found a couple of honest songwriting publishers that helped expose 'Ghost Riders,' and the very first artist to record the song was Burl Ives. Vaughn Monroe released his version of the song before Ives, and it became his biggest hit. Monroe took the song to number one as a pop and western hit, and it stayed on the charts for some fourteen weeks. Over one thousand artists, including Johnny Cash, Marty Robbins and even I, recorded 'Ghost Riders in the Sky.'"

Jones told Western that the first few bars of the song "Ghost Riders" came from the old public domain folk song "When Johnny Comes Marching Home Again." Jones sang, "An old cowpoke went riding out one dark and windy day" in the opening stanza. Stan Jones became a multitalented performer. He also wrote the song "Cowpoke" and the theme to the television western *Cheyenne*.

Out in Hollywood, Jones started working for film director John Ford on some of the magnificent movies Ford shot in Monument Valley, Arizona, and Utah. This led to his writing the theme music to *The Searchers*, starring John Wayne, in 1956. As an interesting side note, singer Buddy Holly got the inspiration to write his big hit "That'll Be the Day" from John Wayne's repeated use of the phrase in the movie. Jones wrote other western theme music for Ford, including for the movies *Wagonmaster* and *Rio Grande*. He even had a small acting part in the latter John Wayne movie.

Jones died of a massive heart attack at the young age of forty-nine in 1963. Stan Jones was one of the most prolific western songwriters of all time and yet another musical icon from Arizona.

10

STUDIOS, LABELS, HONORABLE MENTIONS AND MORE

After successfully launching Sanford Clark, Duane Eddy and others into nationwide and international stardom, Lee Hazlewood had big ambitions to start other record labels, and the VIV imprint was born. His attachment to the label didn't last too long, but he signed many local Phoenix-area players who were aspiring to be stars. Some of those folks included Donnie Owens, Don Cole, Bob Taylor, guitarist Al Casey and Casey's wife, Corki.

Other acts performing in Phoenix and the surrounding area involved with VIV were Jimmy Dell, the Newton Brothers (Wayne and Jerry) and Don Rollins, a songwriter best known for writing "The Race Is On," with which George Jones and others had country hits.

According to the liner notes of the Bear Family boxed set *The VIV Story*, the label released about one hundred single records, no albums and, according to music historian John Dixon, had only one real hit on the *Billboard* charts. That was the top-twenty-five hit from Donnie Owens, "Need You."

The first single to be released on VIV was Jimmy Spellman's "No Need to Cry Anymore" in September 1955. As mentioned in another chapter, Jimmy Spellman became a popular singer and entertainer around the Phoenix valley in that era. The VIV label would continue on after Hazlewood sold it in 1957 to schoolteacher and part-time singer Loy Clingman. Loy, Buddy Wheeler and another partner, Dick Wilson, began construction on a VIV recording studio in 1958 down the street and right around the corner from the iconic Audio Recorders.

Buddy Wheeler also had a music pedigree, having performed on the *Old Dominion Barn Dance* radio show in Richmond, Virginia, and with other country acts. He formed a group called the Westerners, who were backed up by one Marty Robbins before he left the area to be a big star in Nashville at the Grand Ole Opry in the early 1950s.

Wheeler, Clingman and Wilson pooled their resources and started purchasing audio equipment for the new studio. They opened VIV on Indian School Road right across the street from the historic Phoenix Indian School. Shortly after the studio opened, Dick Wilson, also a musician, left for military service and was gone when the session for "Need You" by Donnie Owens was recorded.

It wasn't long before the money ran out, and the VIV studios closed their doors after a little more than two years. Loy Clingman would reopen a more modest VIV studio by enclosing his carport at his home in west Phoenix. Another near-hit record came in 1961 with the song "Scotch and Soda" by Henry Thome. The better-known Kingston Trio's version once again trumped Thome's and became a radio hit, but Thome's version did look promising for a short time, garnering some national and local airplay.

Other artists to grace the VIV studios and record early sides were Mirriam Johnson (Jessi Colter) and the rock group known as the Nazz, which ultimately became Alice Cooper. By the early 1970s, the studio had shut down for good.

Honorable Mention

Many singers and bands recorded music at the VIV studios. The following are a few names of musicians who recorded demos or singles at VIV before it went away: Dal Perkins, Jimmy Johnson, Al Casey and the Arizona Hayriders, Easy Deal Wilson, Eddie LeMaire, the Buffs, Slim Marbles, Faron Warmer, Lonesome John Roller, Don Cole, the Clingman Clan, the Tads, Alvie Self, Corky Casey, Terri and Peggy Edmunson, Jimmy Gray and Jimmy Spellman.

The Dal Perkins band included the cream of the crop of local musicians and players, including Billy Williams, Dick Matheson, Stan Oscarson and Ron Corbin. All would play in various bands in the Phoenix valley. *Courtesy of Ron Corbin and Beve Cole. All rights reserved.*

Mascot Records

In the days of the Phoenix Sound, there were key people who worked to promote the music of the era. Jack Curtis was one of those promotion people. He was described by *Arizona Republic* columnist Dan Nowicki as the "best pal the Phoenix teen community had in those days, as a czar of valley entertainment."

Jack Curtis was a columnist for the *Arizona Republic* from about the late 1950s until 1962. He hosted shows at the Fox Theater and had a local television show. In 1960, he ran teen clubs where kids could hang out and listen to some of the local rock-and-roll bands of that era, including P-Nut Butter, the Vibratos and Frank Fafara.

His first venture was turning the sound stage of Cudia City, a western movie set just north of Camelback Road and Fortieth Street, into a teen club. But it lasted only about ninety days. As the city of Phoenix grew, it encroached on the old movie set. The set was closed, and not a trace of it exists today. Back in the late '50s, Cudia City was the set for the syndicated western television series *26 Men*, which told the story of the famous Arizona Rangers.

Mr. Curtis continued to open clubs in the Phoenix valley, including Stage 7, later renamed the VIP Club, on Seventh Street just up the street from Ramsey's Audio Recorders studio. Like his country music promoter counterpart Ray Odom, Curtis booked many national acts popular in their day, such as Del Shannon, Buffalo Springfield, Dave Clark Five, the Yardbirds and others.

He formed his own record label called Mascot Records and signed acts such as Frank Fafara, Roosevelt Nettles, Jim Boyd, Mike Condello and P-Nut Butter. The Spiders, an early version of the group that would later become Alice Cooper, also recorded some early music on the Mascot label. All of Mascot's recordings were produced at Audio Recorders of Arizona.

By the late 1960s, musical tastes in rock-and-roll were changing, and the last teen club Curtis owned, Beau Brummel's, went out of business.

Porter Sound

There was yet another recording studio in Phoenix in 1957 that turned out some very good music, but not much of it got big exposure anywhere. Porter Records was a small label and studio opened by a former country disc jockey named Frank Porter.

According to liner notes from John P. Dixon on *The Porter Records Story*, a music CD on the German-produced Bear Family Records label, Frank Porter was also known as a local songwriter and had a good ear for music and singers. A parade of local talent recorded on the Porter label. They included local favorite Don Cole, Frank Loren, Rusty Isabell, a group called the Rio Rockers, the Tads, DJ Pete Pepper, Willie Ward, Mark Anthony, the Chamberlain Brothers, the I.V. Leaguers, Billy Adams and Frank Porter himself.

The musical styles ran from rockabilly to country to gospel to good old rock-and-roll. There is a lot of real good music on this CD, much of it not released until the CD's debut in 1998. None of the recorded releases charted nationally, but each act brought a bit of local notoriety and local exposure.

In Tucson, It Was ZOOM Records

One night in 1959, a couple of Tucson, Arizona high school teenagers had an epiphany: "Let's start a record label." Catalina high school friends Ray Lindstrom and Burt Schneider were typical kids getting ready to graduate into the cold, cruel world. They say their interests were radio, records and girls—and probably not in any given order.

Attending a high school "hop," as they called dances in those days, the boys encountered Jack Wallace and the Hi-Tones. This local rock-and-roll group had the audience in the palm of its hand. The girls were screaming as if it was Elvis on stage. Lindstrom and Schneider looked at each other and said, "We've got to record these guys," and the idea for ZOOM Records was born.

In a short time, the boys had recruited the band to a recording session, and within a week, they had cut their first forty-five. Shortly after that, they were getting airplay on the local powerhouse rock station KTKT, where popular Tucson disc jockey Frank Kalil programmed the music. Because Tucson had no recording studio at the time, the guys did their research and headed up the road to Phoenix and Audio Recorders of Arizona. Of course, it didn't hurt that this little studio was having nationwide success with Duane Eddy, Sanford Clark and others.

Lindstrom and Schneider said they were so inexperienced that they started ZOOM Records on a shoe-string budget and never had much more than five dollars at any given time. The boys decided to pool resources and raised thirty-five dollars for that first session with Jack Wallace and the Hi-Tones. They cut "You Are the One" and "I Think of You." Recording and pressing a record was very inexpensive in those days. You could record for about fifteen dollars a session and have your record pressed at the local Wakefield pressing plant over on the Black Canyon Highway.

The next hurdle was promotion and marketing their music and learning how to start their own publishing company. Soon, the boys recruited Pete Ronstadt, who also had a band called the Nightbeats. Ronstadt and his sister Linda also attended Catalina High School. Linda, of course, would go on in the 1970s,

'80s and beyond to have a stellar career in pop music. Pete Ronstadt went on to have a career in law enforcement and was Tucson's police chief for many years.

Ronstadt cut a few sides—including "Lonesome Road Rock," "Nightbeat" and "Doreen"—that received regional airplay in Tucson and other cities. The third music group to record on ZOOM was King Rock and the Knights, who recorded the single "Send-Di," backed with a song called "Scandal."

ZOOM Records' day in the sun was short-lived and had limited success. No one made any money, though it was a learning experience. The boys sent copies of their records to all of the major trade magazines of the day, such as *Billboard* and *Cashbox*. They were pleased to see favorable writeups on many of their songs, but none charted. A couple of the tracks they released garnered some airplay in places like Oklahoma City and Pittsburgh.

Within seven months, ZOOM Records folded as both Schneider and Lindstrom went their separate ways to college and future careers in broadcasting and advertising. ZOOM Records' launch did prove that with ambition and dedication, anything can be accomplished.

Fervor Records: More Players from the Phoenix Sound Era

Moving into the '60s, there were even more singers and bands that recorded in Arizona and attempted to find that elusive hit record. Many acts leaned toward country music, including the heavily Buck Owens–influenced sound of Tommy Strange and the Features; Bozo Darnell; Connie Conway; Jimmy Gray; Mack Fields; Glen Morris; Johnny Appleseed, who reportedly was an early KTUF-KNIX disc jockey; and Jackie Stewart. Phil and the Frantics was another pop act that graced the stage at places like J.D.'s nightclub and recorded in Arizona. Fervor Records, an independent label, has marketed and specializes in these hard-to-find singers and titles. One sample CD is *Vintage Masters, 1957 to 1969*. Fervor also markets much of this music for use in movies and television shows.

Ziggie's Music Store

Along with all of the great music being made in the Phoenix valley from the mid-1950s to the '60s and beyond was a music store that supplied the

A glittering neon sign at Ziggie's Music store, open since 1927 just east of downtown Phoenix. *Courtesy of John Somora Photography and Ziggies Music. All rights reserved.*

working musician with all of the needs of his trade. Ziggie's Music store has been an institution in Phoenix since 1927, when Ziggie Sardus, an accordion player by trade, was passing through town on the way to California. He stopped to visit a relative and apparently never left.

He opened the store during the Depression and began his business selling instruments from guitars to accordions. Scores of musicians, from the solo artist and pick-up garage bands to mariachi bands and country pickers, have patronized the store.

Iconic Phoenix musicians such as Al Casey spent many years teaching young people how to play guitar at the store. Duane Eddy said he purchased his first Gretsch guitar from Ziggie himself in the '50s. In a time when a man's handshake was his bond, Ziggie let Eddy take possession of the guitar before Eddy's dad could stop in and co-sign for the instrument. Eddy paid off the purchase in installments. Trust, and a hand shake, was involved in that transaction.

Ziggie passed away in 1980, and Dionne Hauke, who practically grew up in the store with her grandfather, took possession of the business ten years later, after her grandmother died. Today, the tradition continues of supplying the working musician with the equipment and tools of the trade. The store also continues to offer guitar lessons to locals. The rich heritage business continues to thrive on Third Street just east of downtown Phoenix.

APPENDIX

Bear Family Records has produced two great CDs—*Rockin' and Boppin' in the Desert*, volumes one and two—spotlighting much of the twang, country, rockabilly and flat-out rock-and-roll of the Phoenix Sound era. It's not every song ever recorded, but it offers a nice cross-section and sampling of the music. John P. Dixon wrote the liner notes, which are extensive. Many of these acts received some local radio airplay, and some were never released and sat in a tape vault for years before being dusted off. All were recorded at Ramsey's-Audio Recorders of Arizona, VIV recording studio or Porter Sound in Phoenix.

Rockin' and Boppin' in the Desert,
Arizona Rockabilly, Volume One

Joe Montgomery	Planetary Run	Liberty Bell Records 1957
Al Casey	If I Told You	MCI Records 1956
Bobby Boston	Lazy Dazy	Star-Win Records 1960
Benny Banta	Cry Little Girlie	VIV Records 1959
Billy Barnett	Romp and Stomp	Double B Records 1955
Don Cole	Stop	VIV Records 1958
Dick Robertson & Make Believers	Boppin' Martian	MCI Records 1957

The Tads	Mixed Up Mama	Porter Records 1958
Loy Clingman	Rockin' Down Mexico Way	VIV Records 1960
Jack Lane	King Fool	Yolo Records 1961
Rusty Isabell	Firewater	Brent Records 1959
Lonesome John Roller	Long John's Flagpole Rock	Flagpole Records 1958
Jimmy Dell	Teeny Weenie	RCA Records 1957
Jimmy Johnson & Hayriders	Cat Daddy	VIV Records 1955
Leonard Brothers	Boppin Blue Jeans	VIV Records 1958
Gene Maltais	The Bug	Regal Records 1957
Newton Brothers	Rascal Boogie	Ranger Records 1954
Joe D. Johnson	Rattlesnake Daddy	Acme Records 1957
Doug Harden	Dig That Ford	Liberty Bell Records 1955
Rio Rockers	Mexican Rock 'N' Roll	Capitol / Porter Records 1958
Jim Murphy	I'm Done, Mama	REV Records 1957
Cheek O Vass & Sola Tears	Bo Peep Rock	Twy-Lite Records 1961
Jimmy Gray	Chicksville, USA	Shasta Records 1960
Judy Faye	Rocky Rolly Lover Boy	RCA Records 1957
Duane Turley & Don Cole	Long Gone Cat	VIV Records 1959 Unreleased
Jimmy Patton	Okies in the Pokie	Hilligan Records 1960
Alvie Self	Let's Go Wild	DonRay Records 1959
Bobby & The Demons	The Woo	MCI Records 1960
Q-Zeen	Rain on the Mountain	Yolo Records 1961
Ritchie Hart	The Great Duane	Felsted Records 1959

Rockin' and Boppin' in the Desert, Arizona Rockabilly, Volume Two

Gary LeMel	Rockin' in the Halls	REV Records 1958
Jimmy Bennett & Negligees	Whole Lotta Shakin Goin On	Lancer Records 1963
Rusty Isabell	Morbid Institution	MCI Records 2008 (unreleased)

Jamie Falco & the Red Dots	Stop	MCI Records 2008 (unreleased)
Easy Deal Wilson	Gotta Have You	Sims Records 1959
Jimmy Dell	The Message	RCA Records 1957
George Tyler	I'm Going Back to Texas	Canyon Records 1958
Ron Molina	Esmerella	MCI Records 2008 (unreleased)
The Pledges	Betty Jean	REV Records 1958
The Gigolos	Night Creature	Day Nite Records 1960
Long John Roller	Hey Momma	Flag Pole Records 1959
Waylon Jennings	Rave On	LJR Records 1965
Duane Turley & the Tads	Devil's Den	VIV Records 1959
George Richey	But in a Million Years	Smart Records 1959
The DropOuts	I'm Leaving	Acme Records 1964
Jerry Demar	(She Wants a) Lover Man	Ford Records 1957
The Hawks	A Little More Wine, My Dear	Del Fi Records 1958
Frank Loren	Every One Will Know	Porter Records 1958
Slim Marbles	The Switch	Jo-Ree Records 1962
Niki Sullivan	I Told Everybody	MCI Records 2008 (unreleased).
Al Marion	Kay	Gay Records 2959
Dal Perkins	Kiss Me Goodnight	MCI Records 2008 (unreleased)
Rex Allen Sr.	Knock, Knock Rattle	Decca Records 1956
Jimmy Johnson	How Bout Me, Pretty Baby	VIV Records 1955
Gene Maltais	Lovemakin'	Regal Records 1958
Dick Terry	Mean Bean	MCI Records 2008 (unreleased)
Barry Lane	Oh, Geronimo	Ra-Q Records 1960
Curtis Lee	Pure Love	Warrior Records 1959
Peso Dollar	Sixteen Miles	WBC Records 1961
Ken Patrick	Night Train	Maken Records 1961

Jimmy Silver and the Vagabonds, one of many popular country dance bands in Phoenix in the 1950s. *Courtesy of* True West *magazine and John P. Dixon. All rights reserved.*

The era of the Phoenix Sound was a watershed time of creativity with lots of talented people making their own music, and whether that music was a hit or a miss, it did not matter. All of the music was created by dreamers creating their own art form of rockabilly, country, pop, rock-and-roll, doo-wop, jazz or early soul stylings.

Whether the act was well known or obscure, these recordings and others have become collector's items or have garnered a cult-like following due to the demand for their music and the relative rareness of some of the records.

Grammy Award winner and former Audio Recorders engineer Jack Miller probably summed it up best when he said, "We were there at the beginning just to have fun and make a few bucks. Only later did we realize that collectively we were making a big difference and contributing to the music industry." Jack Miller added, "There also was a caliber of musicians at that particular time in Phoenix that unquestionably was the best I ever encountered. These musicians and singers created the Phoenix Sound in the years between 1957 well into the middle '60s. Even the Beatles were influenced. It was a wonderful time of free musical expression, and it made a big, big impact."

BIBLIOGRAPHY

Chapter 1

D'Andrea, Niki. "Arizona Country Roads." *Phoenix* (July 2014).

Melton, Brad, and Dean Smith. Arizona Goes to War: The Home Front and the Front Lines during World War II. Tucson: University of Arizona Press, 2003.

Shelton, Robert, and Burt Goldblatt, photographer. *The Country Music Story: A Picture History.* Indianapolis, IN: Bobbs-Merrill Co., 1966.

West, Jim. "Arizona Country Music Legends." *Phoenix* (September 2005).

Western, Johnny. Personal interview on Gene Autry, 2012.

Chapter 2

Arizona Music and Entertainment Hall of Fame. Induction, Floyd Ramsey. 2007.

Bio.com. "Lee Hazlewood." http://www.biography.com/people/lee-hazlewood-507259.

Delbridge, Jimmy. Personal interview on Lee Hazlewood, 2011.

Dixon, John P. Personal interview on Floyd Ramsey, 2014.

———. Personal interview on Jack Miller, 2014.

Eddy, Duane. Personal interview on Lee Hazlewood, 2013.

Johnson, Jim, and Lee Hazlewood. *Phoenix Panorama: The VIV Labels.* N.p.: Bear Family Records and John P. Dixon, 1995.

Miller, Jack, of Canyon Records. Personal interview, 2010.

BIBLIOGRAPHY

Chapter 3

Delbridge, Jimmy. Personal interview on Duane Eddy, 2012.

Eddy, Duane. Personal interviews, 2013, 2014.

Gretsch Guitars. "The Duane Eddy Story." YouTube, 2011.

Musical Instrument Museum. "We Are Arizona Music." Phoenix, AZ, 2014.

Rosebrook, Jeb. "Honky Tonk Days in Arizona." *True West* (2011).

Western, Johnny. Personal interview on Duane Eddy, 2012.

Chapter 4

Delbridge, Jimmy. Personal interview, 2012.

Eddy, Duane. Personal interview on Jimmy Delbridge, 2013.

Robinson, Gregory. *Jimmy Dell: God's Grace.* Indianapolis, IN: Noah's Dove Publishing, LLC, 2006.

Rosebrook, Jeb. "Honky Tonk Days in Arizona." *True West* (2011).

Chapter 5

Arizona Music and Entertainment Hall of Fame. Induction Awards and Bio. 2007.

Bennett, Richard. *Al Casey's "Hit List."* Liner notes. Produced by Jack Miller, December 2003.

Dixon, John P. Personal interview on Al Casey, 2012.

Eddy, Duane. Personal interview on Al Casey, 2013.

Hauke, Dionne. Personal interview on Al Casey, 2015.

Miller, Jack. Personal interview on Al Casey, 2010.

Chapter 6

Dixon, John P. Personal interview, 2012.

Madison Square Garden Museum. Phoenix, AZ, 2013.

Odom, Ray. Personal interview, 2012.

Rosebrook, Jeb. "Honky Tonk Days in Arizona." *True West* (2011).

Western, Johnny. Personal interview on Ray Odom, 2012.

BIBLIOGRAPHY

Chapter 7

Arizona Music and Entertainment Hall of Fame. Induction Bio. 2005.

D'Andrea, Niki. "Arizona Country Roads." *Phoenix* (July 2014).

Eddy, Duane. Personal interview on Waylon Jennings, 2013.

Ellis, Dolan. Personal interview on Waylon Jennings, 2015.

Enloe, Professor Karen. "Study: Music of the Southwest." Arizona State University, 2015.

Feiler, Bruce. *Dreaming Out Loud: Garth Brooks, Wynonna Judd, Wade Hayes and the Changing Face of Nashville*. New York: Avon Books, 1998.

Jennings, Waylon. On-air interview. KNIX Radio Phoenix, 1986.

Musical Instrument Museum. "We Are Arizona Music." Phoenix, AZ, 2014.

West, Jim. "Arizona Country Music Legends." *Phoenix* (September 2005).

———. "The Roots of Rock and Roll, Norman Petty Studio." *Route 66* (2003).

Western, Johnny. Personal interview on Waylon Jennings, 2012.

Chapter 8

Allen, Rex, Paula Simpson Witt and Snuff Garrett. *My Life, Sunrise to Sunset*. Scottsdale, AZ: RexGarRuss Press, 1989.

Arizona Music and Entertainment Hall of Fame. Inductee, Dolan Ellis. 2012.

———. Inductee, Johnny Western, 2015.

———. Inductee, Rex Allen Sr., 2007.

Daniels, Larry. "One-on-One Interview with Buck Owens." KTUF-KNIX Radio, 1973.

Dawidoff, Nicholas. *Buck Owens, "Honky Tonk Man": In the Country of Country, Journey to the Roots of American Music*. New York: Vintage Books, Random House, 1998.

Dickens, Little Jimmy. Personal interview on KNIX Radio on the death of Marty Robbins, 1983.

Ellis, Dolan. Personal interview, 2015.

Ellis, Dolan, and Sam Lowe. *Arizona Lens, Lyrics and Lore*. Scottsdale, AZ: Inkwell Books, 2014.

Friends of Marty Robbins Museum. Wilcox, AZ, 2012.

KNIX Radio. Personal interview with Buck Owens, 1982.

Owens, Buddy Alan. Personal interview on Buck Owens, 2007.

Owens, Randy Poe-Buck. *Buck 'Em!: Autobiography of Buck Owens*. Milwaukee, WI: Backbeat Books 2014

Rex Allen Cowboy Museum Research. Wilcox, AZ, 2007.

Robbins, Marizona, wife of Marty Robbins. Personal interview on Marty Robbins's death, 1982.

Robinson, Mamie, and Andrew Means. *Some Memories: Growing Up with Marty Robbins*. N.p.: Booklocker.com, 2007.

Shultz, Larry and Delcie. Personal interview on Rex Allen Sr., 2007.

Western, Johnny. Personal interview, 2011.

Chapter 9

Clemmons, Gary. Personal interview on Buddy Long, 2013.

Cox, Bob, and Tina Cox-Clemmons. Personal interviews on Bob Cox, 2008, 2014.

Fafara, Frank. Personal interview, 2015.

Johnson, Jim, and Lee Hazlewood. *Phoenix Panorama: The VIV Labels*. N.p.: Bear Family Records and John P. Dixon, 1995.

Newman, Ted. Personal interview, 2015.

Self, Alvie. Personal interview, 2014.

Sussman, Terri. Personal interview on Virg Warner and Marty Mitchell, 2015.

Various Artists. *Rockin and Boppin' in the Desert, Arizona Rockabilly*. Vols. 1 and 2. Bear Family Records, with John P. Dixon, 2008.

Warner, Virg. Personal interview on his career, 2015.

Warner, Virg, and Gary Clemmons. Personal interview on Marty Mitchell, 2015.

Western, Johnny. Personal inteview on the life Stan Jones, 2014.

Chapter 10

Curtis, Jack. "Let The Good Times Roll." 2015. http://www.jacks-letthegoodtimesroll.com.

Fafara, Frank. Personal interview on Jack Curtis and Mascot Records, 2015.

Hauke, Dionne. Personal interview on Ziggies Music Store, 2015.

Johnson, Jim, and Lee Hazlewood. *Phoenix Panorama: The VIV Labels*. N.p.: Bear Family Records and John P. Dixon, 1995.

Lindstrom, Ray. Personal interview on ZOOM Records, 2015.

Nowicki, Dan. "Jack Curtis, 'Czar of Valley Entertainment.'" *Arizona Republic* (n.d.).

The Porter Records Story. N.p.: Bear Family Records with John P. Dixon, 1999.

Various Artists. *Rockin and Boppin' in the Desert, Arizona Rockabilly*. Vols. 1 and 2. Bear Family Records, with John P. Dixon, 2008.

———. *Vintage Masters Fervor Records Country 1957 to 1969*. Liner notes. 2007–08.

INDEX

INDEX

INDEX

Y

Yardbirds 109

Z

Ziggie's Music store 36, 49, 111–112
ZOOM Records 110–111

ABOUT THE AUTHOR

Jim West grew up in Tucson, Arizona, the eldest of six children. He began a nearly forty-year broadcasting career while in the U.S. Air Force. That career eventually took him to cities nationwide—such as Indianapolis, Baltimore, Albuquerque, Tucson and Phoenix—and from the island of Guam to the top of the Rockies in Vail, Colorado. Throughout it all, he continued to hone his skills as an on-the-air announcer and then as a program and operations manager. Working for singer Buck Owens at the family-owned KNIX, Phoenix was a career highlight.

Jim has won several ADDY advertising awards for commercial copywriting and has written many articles on music and history for *Route 66* magazine, *AZ-360*, *Pure Country*, *True West* and *Phoenix* magazine.

In addition, Jim served on the ACMA (Academy of Country Music Awards) Board of Directors in Hollywood, helping to plan and execute the yearly network-televised country music awards show.

He was a finalist for CMA (Country Music Association) Large Market Air Personality of the Year and in 2008 was honored by the Phoenix Music Awards with a lifetime achievement award for his contributions to Phoenix radio. As a radio program director, Jim was honored with many Gold and Platinum awards from major record labels.